THE
CORPORATE
PERSON

THE
CORPORATE
PERSON

The nature of volunteer boards,
their culture, and corporate personality

HAROLD EVERSON

Augsburg Fortress
Minneapolis

THE CORPORATE PERSON
The nature of volunteer boards, their culture, and corporate personality

All quotations from the Scriptures, unless otherwise noted, are from the New
Revised Standard Version Bible, copyright © 1989, Division of Christian
Education of the National Council of the Churches of Christ in the United
States of America. Used by permission.

Cover and interior design: Mike Mihelich

AF 34-37196-55535
ISBN 0-8066-3719-6

Manufactured in the U.S.A.
02 01 00 99 98   5 4 3 2 1

CONTENTS

PREFACE

During more than a decade of work with not-for-profit organization governing boards, I've discovered that a central theme continues to emerge in the board development process. It is the concept of the Corporate Person; that is, the corporation as it is embodied in its legally authorized and constituted board of directors.

Working particularly with the church-affiliated social ministry organizations of the Evangelical Lutheran Church in America and one of its predecessor church bodies, The American Lutheran Church, I've learned that no volunteer board is exactly like another. Every one has its own corporate personality and collective culture. Yet, each board is formed by people who come together to envision, think, act, and speak with a common mission, and so grow and work together for the good of a community.

It is for those people that this book is intended. Although developed in the context of my work in training governing boards of organizations entrusted with specific social ministries, I've found the application of many of the concepts described in these pages to be useful for other church-related boards including outdoor ministries, churchwide division boards, and synod and congregational councils. Secular not-for-profit organizations including United Way agencies have also expressed appreciation for the insights that have application to their governance responsibility.

When preparing for work with a board, I always try to visualize this group and ask myself:
- What is this board going to be like?
- How does it behave?
- How does it think?
- How does it communicate?

These are not questions asked about individual board members, but about the board as a single Corporate Person. That Corporate Person is the subject of this book. I offer it to you with the intention that it be used corporately . . . that its ideas be discussed (with the help of questions at the end of each chapter) with other board members who share in the challenging work of volunteer leadership in not-for-profit organizations.

Harold Everson

ACKNOWLEDGMENTS

Over the years, I've had the privilege of dialoguing with many not-for-profit boards about their governance roles and responsibilities. I've chosen to call those dialogues "board seminars" because of the definition of a seminar I once found: "a discussion among experts." We've learned from each other and I've developed a deep respect over the years for volunteer board members who give willingly of their time and energy out of a commitment to the mission, values, and vision of the organizations they govern. To the board members who have participated in my seminars, I'm very grateful.

I'm indebted to the late attorney Eugene Hackler, Olathe, Kan., for some foundational thinking and writing about this concept of the Corporate Person. On many occasions, he set forth the idea of the corporation as a "legal person," tracing its history to its ecclesiastical roots in the Christian church, the Corpus Christi. His insights have laid the groundwork for observations I offer here.

The idea of putting my reflections about boards and the Corporate Person concept into book form emerged from a team of executives and board members who collaborated with me from 1989 to 1992 in board development. These "peer-mentors" provided invaluable feedback and insight: Charles Balcer, Ron Beckman, Richard Borgstrom, Harvey Davis, Helen Frampton, David Helmstetter, Frank Kuhn, Lois Rand, Paul Opgrande, Betty Lou Pyle, Bill Serr, and Tom Steward.

To colleagues in the Evangelical Lutheran Church in America's Division for Church in Society and Lutheran Services in America who have encouraged, prodded, and cheered me on, a special word of thanks: to Charles Miller, executive director of the division; Ruth Reko, director of the leadership development department; and Joanne Negstad, president and CEO, Lutheran Services in America; for their affirmation and support and for helping me frame my sabbatical writing goals and enthusiastically holding me to them; to Kurt Reichardt, who gave generously of his editing skills and constructive comment; and to Karen Peterson, my support staff person, who spent countless hours at the word processor patiently deciphering my scribbling and putting edits and rewrites into legible form.

And most of all, to Dorothy, my wife (and proofreader extraordinaire, who has meticulously read and reread the manuscript of this book): My board development work has meant hours of preoccupation with the subject, and many days, many weekends, away from home. Although she would readily admit that she neither needs nor wants to know a lot about boards or governance, her interest, encouragement, and prayers have sustained me constantly. She is indeed the heart and soul of the Corporate Person we two have become through the years of our life together.

1 ORIGINS

The corporation is "an artificial being, invisible, intangible, and existing only in contemplation of law. Being a mere creature of law, it possesses only those properties which the charter of its creation confers upon it."

Chief Justice John Marshall
Dartmouth College case, 1819

There is a wonderful, if somewhat archaic, bit of legal jargon in the articles of incorporation of some not-for-profit corporations, with words to this effect:

> The corporation shall have the capacity to act, possessed by natural persons, but it shall have authority to perform only acts that are necessary and proper to accomplish its purposes and not repugnant to law. . . . All directors shall be natural persons.

Upon coming across a set of governing documents worded like that, the casual reader might well ask, "A corporation and its board made up of 'natural persons?' One would certainly hope so! If not 'natural' persons, then what?"

The answer to that question is not "un-natural persons," but rather, "an artificial person." Collectively, that's the way the law has defined the corporation—*a single legal entity, an artificial being, created by the state for a specific and limited purpose*. To incorporate means to create a body or corpus that in the eyes of the law is every bit as legitimate and real as flesh and blood.

CORPUS CHRISTI AND ROMAN CULTURE

Incorporation is a concept that grew out of the Christian theological principle of the Corpus Christi, the "body of Christ," a way in which the Christian church has traditionally defined itself.[1] The twelfth chapter of 1 Corinthians is central to this principle. Ironically, the link between the Corpus Christi and the word "incorporate" (to "form one body") seems to be forgotten by some in the church today. For them the words "corporate" and "corporation" carry only negative connotations of greed, power, avarice, and injustice—images of huge multinational for-profit power structures designed only to exploit and oppress. But the church would do well to rediscover its corporate heritage and its involvement in the development of the not-for-profit corporation, and from that history reclaim its understanding of what it means to live and work corporately as one body—the body of Christ. That's true not only for boards of church-related not-for-profit organizations, but for members of congregations that are themselves incorporated.

There are lessons to be learned as well from the secular corporate world, which has developed sophisticated rules and processes for governing and decision making—lessons the church can appropriate and reclaim as fundamental to leadership for the common good.

The concept of the Corpus Christi was used by the thirteenth-century Pope Innocent IV to form local parish corporations in England.[2] But historically—and biblically—the concept of the Corporate Person long pre-dates the advent of the corporation as we know it today. An understanding of the Old and New Testament perceptions of community provides some insights:

> Biblically, it is not possible to separate Christians as individuals from the church seen as a community of faith. Indeed, it is unlikely that such a notion could have been conceived of before the emergence of individualism in eighteenth-century secular thought. In the Hebrew Bible, the sense of communal solidarity is so strong that proper nouns, apparently singular, are actually plural in intent. Thus, the Hebrew conception of corporate personality as expressed in the covenant tradition assumes that the human factor with which Yahweh has to deal is not a collection of individuals, much less an utterly solitary individual, but a people bound together in a common history and called to obedience in a shared destiny.[3]

Ancient societies that pre-date the Hebrews also held the fundamental notion of the corporate group taking precedence over that of individuals. The idea that families and tribes had an existence over and above that of their individual members reflected a kind of corporate understanding of an existence that perpetuated itself in a permanent succession through generations.

The concept of an organization with a collective membership of natural persons whose life continued beyond that of any one natural person was in place before the advent of Christianity. It began to take shape in the Greek city states and the Roman Empire. In Roman law, the most commonly used expression for the idea of the Corporate Person was *universitas personarum*, that is, an "aggregate of persons." The highest example of a *universitas personarum* was the Roman state itself. There were also others—such as municipalities and private societies—to which the law had expressly given recognition and legitimacy, along with corporate privileges.

There was a fundamental principle in the creation of a *universitas personarum*. It could not come into being simply by the act or decision of a group of individuals. It had to have its existence conferred upon it by the charter of the state, giving it status in the eyes of the law as a separate artificial person with rights and responsibilities.

The *universitas personarum* in the pre-Christian Roman Empire had three chief characteristics very similar to the rules in Anglo-American law governing corporations today. They were that:

- the corporate body has an existence independent of its members.
- the members may die or resign and others take their place, but the body has a continuing existence.
- the corporate body may possess common property and a common purse distinct from that of its members. (Debts, therefore, due to or by the corporate body are not debts due to or by the individuals composing it.)[4]

It's fascinating to speculate about the extent to which the concept and characteristics of *universitas personarum* influenced the emerging Christian church in Roman society.[5] The New Testament word for church, a rendering of the Greek *ekklēsia*, was the term used in Greek city states for the assembly of citizens summoned for legislative purposes.[6] "It is interesting to note that the Roman world did not even try to translate the word *ekklēsia*; it simply transliterated it into *ecclesia* and used it in the same way."[7]

Obviously, there was a link to the culture of the day in the use of *ecclesia* to describe the organization of the early church. There is little doubt that the cultural milieu of the Roman Empire provided the environment in which the church was nurtured. St. Paul was a Roman citizen familiar with Rome's political structure, and it is probably more than coincidental that the characteristics of the *universitas* are strikingly similar to descriptions of the emerging church in passages of New Testament scripture. For example:

"Now you are the body of Christ, and individually members of it" (1 Corinthians 12:27). *The body has an existence independent of its members.*

"And I tell you, you are Peter, and on this rock I will build my church, and the gates of death will not prevail against it" (Matthew 16:18 RSV). *The members may die or resign, others taking their place, but the body has a continuing existence.*

"Now the whole group of those who believed were of one heart and soul, and no one claimed private ownership of any possessions, but everything they owned was held in common" (Acts 4:32). *It may possess common property and a common purse distinct from that of its members.*

Perhaps the primary thing the first-century church lacked to become a *universitas personarum* was the recognition and charter of the Roman state. While that would have politically legitimatized the body of Christ, the "followers of the way," the *ecclesia*, it was something neither the government nor the early Christians desired or demanded. On the contrary, the early church was considered a *religio illicita* (an illegitimate religious community) by the government, which held there could be no worship of God apart from the state. Since Christians believed that was idolatry and refused to take part in the state worship, their organization was proscribed and persecuted.

The church was first recognized by the Roman state under the emperor Gallienus in A.D. 260, not as a *universitas* but as a *religio illicita*. That status lasted for 40 years after which the Roman emperor Diocletian made an empire-wide concerted effort to annihilate the church. Finally, in A.D. 313, the edict of the emperor Constantine, a convert to Christianity, gave formal recognition to the Christian church, not as a *universitas personarum*—a state-chartered organization among others—but as the *ecclesia universalis*, the religion of the Holy Roman Empire.

THE EMERGENCE OF THE CORPORATE PERSON

While the Christian church continued to develop St. Paul's theological concept of itself as "one body with many members" (1 Corinthians 12:12), it remains an unsettled question among scholars of corporate history whether or not the Romans conceived of their form of secular organization as a separate legal person.[8] Incorporation as a legal process came only following the decline of the Roman Empire, and from very pragmatic need—that of determining land ownership by the church in medieval England.

". . . the church appears to have been the most direct link between Roman legal views of organization and those developed in English common law. Church property had come to be considered as separate and distinct from the natural person who held office. The opposition of the church to free incorporation was crystallized by Pope Innocent IV, who reigned from 1243 to 1254, and regarded the church as having the exclusive privilege of granting such charters. Kings began to grant corporate privileges to towns and nonreligious organizations, so that the notion of a grant of power from a sovereign authority became established."[9]

Eugene Hackler describes the emergence of the corporation this way:

In the early days, the ownership of land led to a concern about what the congregation was. The early English law called the church land "God's property and the church's twelve-fold." The "saints" were the administrators. The ownership of all church land was in the Pope. In order to achieve centralized ownership in Rome, it was said that in church property "geography must yield to law." The concept of [papal] ownership of the church was that the church particular (*ecclesia particularis*) was conceived as a part and member of the church universal (*ecclesia universalis*). The parochial church, by this reasoning, became a "member of the body." By legal fiction, the church was a person and the local parish was considered a member of the "body." The canonists and philosophers treated the church as a person—"the body and bride of the Redeemer."

Men and women began to worry about who owned and who would handle church property. So the . . . church lawyers and philosophers got together and they said, "What can we do about this title to land?" They said that they really needed some new legal vehicle for church property. They reasoned that it was proper to give the congregation title to church land, but not to individuals. They resolved that congregations are the "body and bride of the Redeemer," being a "corpus" (body) and therefore they should incorporate, i.e. create a legal body. The word corporation comes from the word "corpus." When the early church lawyers decided to create a legal body, the corporation was born.[10]

And so too was the idea of the Corporate Person. Though it remained for the legal evolution of the idea to be developed in English common law and American corporate law, the concept of the Corporate Person had its genesis within the church.

One further observation regarding the origins and development of the Corporate Person should be noted. If the corporation is that artificial person defined by law, then the governing board of the corporation is the embodiment/incarnation of that artificial person.[11] The board—which exists by authorization of the corporate members—is the actual living, breathing, thinking, acting, flesh-and-blood entity that represents the corporate owners, members, and stakeholders who comprise and surround the corporation. In turn, the members limit their control and agency by conferring them to the board. They delegate the board to act on their behalf. Since it exists at the will of the corporate members who elect it, the board is therefore understood by the state to be the ultimately responsible *person*.[12] (Note: In the case of self-perpetuating boards with no corporate members but themselves, the board in essence is the corporation and acts on its own will.)

The essential point is that the corporation, as embodied and personified by its board, is to be seen as a single, separate person with its own will. It has the right to act independently within the limits established by its charter and articles of incorporation. The Corporate Person is a term used to describe:

1. the legal status of a corporation and its board.
2. the mind-set of individuals on that board.

The challenge to board members as individuals is to learn to think and act together as that Corporate Person. The following chapters will describe some of the ramifications of that challenge in rather anthropomorphic terms: corporate body, soul, mind, behavior, voice, and health.

QUESTIONS FOR DISCUSSION
CHAPTER 1: ORIGINS

1. The church would do well to rediscover its corporate heritage and its involvement in the development of the not-for-profit corporation, and from that history reclaim its understanding of what it means to live and work corporately as one body. (p. 1)

    A. What is your understanding of the word corporation? What connotations does it carry for you?
    B. When you think of your organization as a corporation, what images come to mind?
    C. As a board member of a corporation, how is the biblical concept of "many members, one body" helpful to you in your relation to other members of your board?

2. If the corporation is that artificial person defined by law, then the governing board of the corporation is the embodiment/incarnation of that artificial person. (p. 5)

    A. If the state creates and gives legitimacy to a corporation as an artificial person, what does being a part of that artificial person as a board member of your corporation mean to you?
    B. Review the articles of incorporation of your not-for-profit corporation. What does this document say about the legal status of your organization, its purposes and limitations, and the authority of your board?

2 BODY

Indeed, the body does not consist of one member but of many. . . . If one member suffers, all suffer together with it; if one member is honored, all rejoice together with it.

St. Paul, 1 Corinthians 12:14, 26

Who is this Corporate Person—the board, the embodiment of the corporation—anyway? First impressions are significant. First impressions are often drawn from physical appearance and body language; that is, how the body looks and acts.

At the outset, one could be clinical about the corporate body and spend time examining its pedigree and papers. After all, the Corporate Person's birth certificate is its articles of incorporation. They describe the body's legal status, purpose, and limitations. But this body is more dynamic than that. It's a complex organism made up of many members who interact, create tensions and stresses, push and pull, and hopefully work together to get things done. Rather than by examining pedigrees and papers, we begin to learn who the body is by *observing it in action.*

Richard O. Scherch, in describing a systems approach to voluntary organizations, draws the analogy to the human body this way:

> It is a system that has a specific goal or set of goals that enables the individual to function successfully. One of the goals is to walk forward. In so doing, many parts of the system must interact—the feet, the limbs, the head, the eyes, the ears, the muscles, and so on. Each of them has a separate objective. The ear, for example, helps maintain balance. The eyes establish direction, tracking where the system is going. The muscles move the limbs: the legs, as the agents of locomotion, and the arms for assistance in balance—different objectives, the same goal.[1]

The significance of how the body works is not in the homogeneity of its members, but in the way those members work together toward a common goal. In the language of today's not-for-profit corporation, the essential dynamic is a commitment to a common mission. That's the heartbeat, passion, and energy of the corporate body.[2] At least it ought to be.

Dysfunctional systems

There are a few dysfunctional boards where the members go to meetings as if they are going off to war against their executive, some particular issue, or simply against each other. It's a behavior pattern that becomes ingrained in their culture, a kind of negative body language. It may begin with the attitude of one or more members who don't understand the old adage "You can disagree without being disagreeable." However, it may also be deeper than that and arise from the fact that some members of the body insist on their own autonomy, or maintain a loyalty to some theory, political philosophy, or constituent group. It may simply be that the satisfaction of their own egos takes precedence over a commitment to the organization's mission.

Board development expert John Carver has made the observation that "the board as a body is obligated to protect itself and its staff from the board as individuals."[3] Consider that statement in the context of a comment from John Gardner's book, *On Leadership*:

> The war of the parts against the whole is the central problem of pluralism today. Thus our capacity to frustrate one another through non-cooperation has increased dramatically. The part can hold the whole system up for ransom.[4]

When that happens, the body becomes crippled and ineffective. It is unable to focus on its mission and goals because it is preoccupied with the pain being caused by one or more of its members.

It doesn't take an intense scrutiny of a board's body language to know whether the body is hobbled or hurting. One symptom is the presence of either or both the "omnipotent" or "omnipresent" board member. These are people who understand neither the legal nor the functional limitations of the Corporate Person.

The omnipotent board member takes upon himself or herself the power of the board, without understanding that the power of individual board members is limited to what they do corporately. Their power is exercised within legally called meetings, or when delegated by the corporate body to act with authority outside of those meetings as individuals or committees of the board.

The basic principle that is missed by these omnipotent board members is "Without the board, you're not the board." That is not an easy principle for some members to learn or practice, particularly in a day and age where individualism and autonomy are highly valued. For skilled, talented, professional people who are vocationally accustomed to leading and acting as responsible decision makers, the shift to being a volunteer member of a body that must think, act, and decide corporately instead of unilaterally may be a difficult challenge. "Without the board, you're not the board" means relinquishing some personal power on behalf of strengthening the body. It means recognizing that the vigor and vitality of the board comes from the combined wisdom and abilities of its individual members acting as a collaborative team with a common mission and common goals. It's the principle of synergy.

The same symptoms of dysfunction are manifested by the presence of the omnipresent board member. This member is the micromanager who can't make the distinction between the board's governance role and the staff's operational role. John Carver has noted that "what may be responsible behavior in a job may be irresponsible behavior on a board. A 'detail person' may be excellent in his/her employment . . . but probing into every detail of administration may be irresponsible as a board member."[5]

Obviously, board members need to take personal interest and get involved in the organization they govern. They need to be concerned about the health of the corporate body. However, there is a fine line between governing and meddling, and the rule of thumb for members of the corporate body is to mind your own business.[6] That simply means that board members need to know what is the business of the board and what is that of the staff. As board members, they need to give their full attention and energy to providing corporate oversight and accountability through planning, monitoring, evaluating, and policy making. It also means that, while supporting the work they do, they must refrain from hovering over administration and staff and stay out of internal management struggles.[7]

Another symptom of the hurting or hobbled corporate body is the presence of "impotent/irrelevant" members. Their behavior is just the opposite of omnipotent or omnipresent members. The damage impotence and irrelevance does to the body is most evidenced by board members who are frequently absent from meetings. There really is no such thing as an excused absence. If a member is not at a meeting—excused or not—a part of the body is missing. By the same token, members who attend meetings but never express ideas or opinions or ask questions only contribute to board dysfunction. Members whose only contributions are to second motions, move for adjournment, and make small talk before and after meetings are not people who relevantly contribute to the life of the corporate body.

At this point, two observations are important for comprehending the board as a corporate body. The first is to understand that the board is chosen to fulfill a trust responsibility on behalf of others. It is to ask hard questions and make good decisions without referring every difficult issue to a plebiscite or a referendum of the corporate members, stakeholders, or constituents.

That doesn't mean that timely consultation and information gathering aren't important. It does mean that board members are obliged to exercise independent judgments when decisions are needed. They are not to be just rubber stamps for the wishes of certain constituents or clients. If liability should result from a board decision, it is the board as a body that will be responsible, not the corporate members.[8] One of the primary reasons the corporation is formed is to limit the liability of the corporate members. That responsibility is conferred upon the board as a body by the members of the corporation, who in so doing relinquish control and agency.[9]

The second observation is that the board as a body is incomplete without the executive leader, the arms and legs of the organization. The Corporate Person can accomplish its goals only when there is capable administrative leadership working on a day-to-day basis. Trust, communication, integrity, and a clear understanding of board and staff roles are essential elements in this collaborative relationship. The kindest thing the board as a body can do for itself is to hire an effective executive, then nurture that relationship not in a top-down authoritarian manner, but in a clear partnership.

THE BODY'S QUALITY OF LIFE

As described in chapter 1, one of the characteristics of the Corporate Person is that "the members may die or resign and others take their place, but the body has a continuing existence." Given that reality, the quality of life of the body is a vital concern and responsibility of the board. Since so much time and effort has been invested by members in the life of the organization, board members need to protect that investment with carefully delineated policies and processes. That is true not only for the nomination of new members, but for an entire spectrum of activities devoted to the life, health, and growth of the Corporate Person.

Care and concern for body building is necessary both for boards that are organized on a self-perpetuating basis and those elected by a corporate membership. As a matter of fact, many self-perpetuating boards are less than healthy, precisely because they are often without policies for board rotation and limitation of terms, and there is little involvement in the selection process from their constituencies and communities. They risk becoming entrenched, myopic clubs, with little vision and few new ideas.

Quality in the life of the corporate body has four clear elements:

Personal dimension
The first element of board quality is the personal dimension and its components: individual commitment, a sense of self-worth, and a desire for excellence.

Without commitment on the part of board members, the body suffers. When one or more members are not committed to the mission of the organization and service to the organization's community and constituents, the rest of the body is cheated, short-changed, and crippled.

Quality board members have sufficient self-esteem to know that they have gifts to be used, and they are willing to make contributions of their time, expertise, energy, teamwork, and support.

Finally, there is a desire for excellence. The Corporate Person needs to have a vision and high expectations for the organization. Pity the poor executive or other staff who must constantly be challenging the corporate body to look forward rather than backward, or who must continually drag the board along like so much dead weight!

Legal dimension

The second element of board quality is the legal dimension. This Corporate Person has a body that is a creature of law. Consequently, the body must be made up of members who will function legally. That is, they will recognize an obligation to be accountable by observing the *duty of care*, meaning they will act with prudent judgment in handling the affairs of the organization. Moreover, they will assume a fiduciary responsibility, the *duty of loyalty*, by acting in good faith, being scrupulous about duality, nepotism, and other conflicts of interest. Finally, the Corporate Person as a body will practice the *duty of obedience*, observing the limitations imposed by law and the rules that require working together as members of the body. (See chapter 5 for more on legal responsibility.)

Monsignor Charles Fahey of Fordham University, commenting on the legal dimension of board quality, has said that "board members . . . exist, before the law, as groups who say they do what is described as the purpose of their organization in its articles of incorporation. [They are] to see that this purpose is carried out both before the law and before the community they serve, which has placed them in the position of trust."[10]

Ethical dimension

The third element of board quality is the ethical dimension. Beyond the legal requirements of the corporate body, board members of not-for-profit organizations need to see themselves as servants acting with a public trust, and that means acting ethically. Monsignor Fahey again:

> We raise our children to do more than just what the law demands; not to be moral only to the extent that you won't get caught . . . or to be only as lawful as the law presumes you to be. Do our organizations only concern themselves with measuring up to minimum standards . . . and doing that

which one can get away with for the sake of expediency—or do we act on a higher ethical level than that? Our organizations ought not only to be legal. They ought to be virtuous as well.[11]

In considering the ethical dimension in the quality of the Corporate Person, a paraphrase of a comment by Voltaire is worth reflecting upon: "The prudent person does himself [herself] good; the virtuous person does good to others." That's as true for the Corporate Person as it is for individuals. Members of the body ought not only be guided by the negative ethical maxim "do no harm." They ought to seek to do good—to others.

Spiritual dimension

The fourth element is less tangible, and not equally applicable to all organizations. But for many not-for-profit boards there is a spiritual—even theological—dimension that moves, motivates, and gives quality of life to the body. It may simply grow out of the members' common sense that in some undefined way they are doing good for more than simply humanitarian reasons. Better yet, the board may be vigorously guided by a strong and clearly articulated set of values/theological principles that delineate its work as serving in response to the will and love of God. If the corporate body has been created from that motivation and for that purpose, it's a dimension that needs to be embraced by the members. It is a powerful force that gives life to the body.[12]

STRENGTHENING THE CORPORATE BODY

How does the body grow and gain strength? First of all, it must take proactive responsibility to see that its quality of life is maintained. To accomplish that, some boards have established active, year-round board development or governance committees, often expanding the job description of the traditional nominating committee.

This committee initially addresses the definition of the quality and characteristics to be sought in board members. It also develops and maintains job descriptions for them and maintains—for future reference—an ongoing file of potential board members. That file is drawn upon to recommend and recruit board nominees for full and unexpired terms as board vacancies occur. This committee may also be authorized to plan and conduct orientation sessions for new members, nominate board officers, coordinate ongoing board development activities, and lead an annual self-assessment and evaluation of the life and health of the body. The committee may even tend to such details as tracking board member terms; maintaining policies relating to board attendance, indemnification, and directors' and officers' insurance; and monitoring legislative activity relating to volunteerism, liability, and tax exempt status issues.

Andrew Swanson, writing in one of his *Board Sense* papers about the way boards are developed, observes that:

> The concentration seems to be upon offering nostrums designed to make disparate groups of people somehow work better together as a board . . . [when] the very first concern . . .ought to be about the process by which the board was assembled in the first place! Many, if not most, of the ills which beset some voluntary boards would dry up and blow away if the selection process were made the primary concern and given the attention it deserves.[13]

Within the corporation, there is an investment to protect. Who knows better than an incumbent board what type of new members the board needs in order to fill vacant positions? While board members ought not to name their own successors or try to steer the election process, the board's input into the nominating process is vital in terms of defining clearly the criteria for maintaining the Corporate Person's quality of life. New members of the body need to be as strong or stronger than those leaving the body, and they need to have the right qualifications.

It's a large but crucial job when it comes to building the body. The Corporate Person is an aggregate of its members. The size and composition of that body have much to do with its strength.[14] Often the question is asked "How large should a board be?" The general rule of thumb is "large enough to represent its constituents; small enough to be effective and efficient."

Who should serve on a board? Diversity and inclusiveness are the key words today. Diversity means a mix of women and men who are part of the constituency being served. There should be a racial and ethnic balance with varied educational, social, and economic levels represented, together with a variety of skills, perspectives, and backgrounds. These important factors all bring richness and strength to the board, though they should not be wielded with a legalistic Noah's ark (two of every kind of creature) mentality.

The board, using the principle of diversity, should seek members who will provide the body with essential skills and strengths including good business sense and financial judgment, the ability to listen and participate appropriately, and a willingness to work as part of a team. It needs to look for members who demonstrate positive attitudes, compassion for people, a sense of servant leadership, and a commitment to the mission of the organization. Though different members have different abilities and skills in differing amounts, they all contribute to the strength and functioning of the body. The key is balance, coordination, mutual effort, and a clear vision.

QUESTIONS FOR DISCUSSION
CHAPTER 2: BODY

1. The basic principle is ... "Without the board, you're not the board."
   (p. 9)

   A. If members of the board on which you serve must restrict them-
      selves to decision making within legally called meetings, how would
      you deal with a situation in which one or two members habitually
      attempt to make decisions outside board meetings, without board
      authorization?

   B. Have you ever known board members who display symptoms of
      omnipotence, omnipresence, or irrelevance? How has that type of
      behavior affected the well-being of the corporate body?

2. The quality of life of the body is a vital concern and responsibility of
   the board. (p. 11)

   A. How do the personal qualities of commitment, self-worth, and a
      desire for excellence manifest themselves among the members of
      your board?

   B. Can you cite examples of "prudent judgment," "acting in good
      faith," and the "duty of obedience" in the actions and decision mak-
      ing of your board? What would breaches of those legal obligations
      do to the quality of life of your board?

   C. How does your board, as a body, value the ethical commitment to
      "being good and doing good" as a fundamental quality of the corpo-
      rate person? How have your board's ethics been challenged or tested?

   D. What evidences of a spiritual dimension add quality to your corpo-
      rate body?

3. How does the body grow and gain strength? First of all, it must take
   proactive responsibility to see that its quality of life is maintained.
   (p. 13)

   A. How are your board members chosen? What intentional processes
      are used to strengthen the corporate body in that selection process?

   B. What demonstrates diversity on your board now? How do you see
      diversity strengthening the body?

   C. In what ways does your board nurture its corporate body?

3 SOUL

Does the Corporate Person have a soul? Is there some spiritual reality, some unseen and intangible force in the corporate body that shapes its will, inspires commitment, and instills a passion for action?

If the ethical and theological dimensions of board quality shape the Corporate Person's thinking and behavior, then there is indeed an inherent spiritual reality, a soul, a "breath of life," that determines whether an organization simply exists, or really lives.

Four words with distinct spiritual connotations describe the essence of the Corporate Person's soul: *vision*, *values*, *mission*, and *conscience*. When a group of individuals comes together as a corporate body, its focus needs to be on what is best for the body, not what is best for any one or two members. The individual members need to see and understand why the body exists, and discover and be committed to the meaning of its life. In other words, the Corporate Person needs the ability to see (vision), to believe (values), and to act (mission) with integrity (conscience).

There are some clear links between the corporate soul and the pragmatic outcome of the goals the corporate body is seeking to accomplish. The linkage looks like this:

1. Commitment is based on clear vision.
2. The clearer the vision, the stronger the commitment.
3. The stronger the commitment, the greater the possibility the organization will reach its goals.

When it is clear and understood, there is something almost mystical about a common vision within the corporate soul. It has an ability to bring a diverse group of individuals together, and a power to inspire results. A primary reason why the United States was able to land men on the moon in 1969 was that the vision for accomplishment was so clear. The moon was there—visible and shining for all to see—and people understood the challenge. President Kennedy's 1960 mission statement was simple and to the point. It was to land astronauts on the surface of the moon and bring them back safely by the end of the decade. It challenged and unified people to accomplish a seemingly impossible task. Would that every challenge facing every organization be envisioned so clearly!

Granted, solutions to the social issues and problems most not-for-profit organizations deal with don't lend themselves to such specific definition. However, when people wring their hands and shake their heads over the fact that we can land on the moon but we can't solve problems on earth, they are getting at the heart of what is at issue. Too often there is a lack of clear vision for what needs to be accomplished, or if there is some vision it isn't widely enough shared.

Martin Luther King's "I Have A Dream" speech galvanized thousands of people in the cause of justice, equality, and freedom. But it still remains for the corporate soul of America—its government, churches, and organizations—to widely share that vision. Though the motto of the United States is *e pluribus unum*—from many, one—it hasn't yet captured America's corporate soul.

VISIONING: SHAPING THE FUTURE

"From many, one" describes the way the Corporate Person needs to function. In not-for-profit governing boards, where many of the issues and concerns of society and community are addressed, the bonding power of a common vision is absolutely essential. Unfortunately, the process of visioning, especially as the joint activity of the corporate body, is something of a lost art. In ordering priorities, it is often too easily relegated to the bottom of the list. The regular business of the board, time constraints on its volunteer members, the state of constant change in which organizations live, and just plain confusion about what a "vision" is, all contribute to inertia in visioning.

Visioning needs to be an ongoing concern, a collaborative effort of the board and executive leadership. It deals with questions of purpose, future, and a sense of direction. Too many boards spend unproductive time on where they've been. They dwell on reports of completed program objectives, financial printouts of money already spent, updates on fund-development dollars already raised, and executive reports of accomplished activities. While important information, much of this could better be submitted in writing in advance of meetings. That way, the Corporate Person (the board in its meetings) can give primary attention to thinking, planning, and visioning for the future.

In working with board development, I've sometimes used this analogy: Some board meetings are like a group of decision makers piling into a van to go for a ride, with the executive at the steering wheel. Once under way, most of them—preoccupied with where they've been—spend time either looking out the rear window or at the rearview mirrors. A few study the scenery through the side windows as it goes by. They're the ones who want to know what's happening now. Unfortunately, only one or two in the front seat take responsibility for looking through the windshield to see what's ahead, reading the road maps, and offering the driver directions for the best way to reach their destination. They're the ones with vision, something that is always better than 20/20 hindsight. (Oh yes, there may be a passenger who now and then insists on leaning over to help the driver with the operational business of steering the van and that can be disastrous!)

The point is this: the business of the board is to look ahead, and that begins with visioning. Then it means articulating the vision through planning and policy making, a process that requires some soul searching on the part of the Corporate Person. Donald R. Johnston, a health care consultant from Spokane, Wash., puts it well:

> To develop a vision that will sustain an organization in the future, [board members] must collaborate and engage in a dialogue. Time must be devoted to developing a commonly shared vision. This process presents a good opportunity for board members to get to know one another well, to explore one another's values and views. Often, trustees make decisions based on implied, assumed values or standards of other trustees on the board. But values, views, ethical standards of each trustee must be explicitly shared and explored if the board is to develop a genuinely shared value statement.[1]

DEFINING CORPORATE VALUES

The Corporate Person's belief system is understood through common values. Defining those values undergirds the vision of the organization. It begins with individual members of the body describing to others their own values and beliefs. Max De Pree, chairman of Herman Miller, describes the philosophy of his organization:

> We understand that the corporation is an entity only in that it is an expression of each of us as individuals. We know that the soul and spirit, the gifts, the heart and dignity of each of us combine to give the corporation these same qualities. . . . Shared ideals, shared ideas, shared goals, shared respect, a sense of integrity, a sense of quality, a sense of advocacy, a sense of caring—these are the basis of Herman Miller's covenant and value system. Our system of values may not be generic. It must be explicit. The system and the covenant around it make it possible for us to work together, not perfectly to be sure, but nevertheless in a way that enables us to have the potential to be a gift to the spirit.[2]

The values listed by De Pree are the core beliefs of his organization. Similarly, each governing board—together with its executive leader—must determine what value words best describe the beliefs of its corporate soul.[3] What is said about those value words reflects the beliefs the members agree upon. In turn, this becomes a common basis for corporate vision and mission, and a guide for the corporate conscience. Values statements are the moral fiber and spiritual strength of the Corporate Person.

How are values defined and articulated corporately? In my work with boards, I've found this five-step values identification process useful for not-for-profit organizations that provide services to people:

Step 1 asks the group to list the services the organization provides and the kind of work it does.

Step 2 calls for the group to envision the future, listing the challenges that will need to be addressed in terms of work to be done and services to be provided.

Step 3 analyzes both current tasks and future challenges, asking "With what issues and problems do the lists generated from steps 1 and 2 deal?" From this analysis a list of generally negative issues— loneliness, illness, isolation, injustice, and so forth—is developed.

Step 4 asks the group to take each negative issue that surfaced in step 3 and state its opposite; that is, the positive outcome or response the organization seeks to achieve. These positives begin to describe the values of the organization.

Step 5 gets to the heart of the organization's values by asking, "What are the reasons for seeking these positive outcomes? What motivates the effort? What values drive the activity of our organization?"

After step 5, boards are asked to reexamine and rephrase their value statements to the point where there is common agreement, acceptance, and commitment by all members and the executive leader. This set of values statements, established as policy, reflects the soul of the Corporate Person. It serves as an inspiration and motivation for staff, clients, constituents, and the community the organization serves. Clear vision—based on clearly defined values—inspires commitment, and commitment produces action.

MISSION MOTIVATION

How are vision and values, the soul of the Corporate Person, communicated? The operative word is *mission*. Out of those belief statements, which may be fairly lengthy and sometimes a bit ponderous, need to come a brief, concise, focused statement that can move people to action. The statement needs to speak of purpose and reason for being. It needs to say what business the organization is about and it needs to say that in a way that is different from the often colorless phrasing of the organization's purpose statement found in the articles of incorporation.

The mission statement needs to have passion. It needs to go to the heart of the organization's values and focus on its clear vision. Mission statements ought to be short and to the point. They need to possess a strong emotional component, and be linked to visible actions that everyone in the organization—board, executive leadership, and staff—can affirm and endorse. As Peter Drucker has said, "[Not-for-profit organizations] exist for the sake of their mission . . . and this must never be forgotten. The first task . . . is to make sure that everybody sees the mission, hears it, lives it."[4]

Mission "describes the human face of the organization . . . how it is lived out and the image it reflects to the public. . . . Mission is a frame of mind" for the Corporate Person.[5]

Some years ago, I saw mission at work in an exemplary manner in a purely secular and proprietary setting. I flew to Des Moines, Iowa, for a meeting that was to be held at the University Park Holiday Inn. I called for airport transportation from the hotel's courtesy phone in the terminal, and very promptly was met at the curbside by their van. The driver loaded my luggage, and as we drove across town he asked if I had ever been at the inn. When I told him this was my first visit to Des Moines, he replied, "I think you're really going to like it!" My somewhat travel-worn skepticism surfaced as I thought to myself, "You've been well-trained in public relations, young man."

But he was right. I did like it. When we arrived, there were doormen (two of them!) to greet me and bring my bags to the desk. The registration clerk had check-in forms ready for my signature and gave me directions to my room. The ambiance of the lobby was wonderful. It included a plant-filled atrium, a beautiful decor, and a glass-enclosed elevator to take me to the third floor.

As I stepped into the elevator, thinking I would look out over the lobby on my way up, something caught my eye. Just inside the door was a brass plaque, engraved with the mission statement of the hotel:

We are dedicated to service and product excellence.
We truly believe the guest is our first concern.
To substantiate this philosophy we will maintain a positive and motivated environment for our cast members (employees).
Our commitment to these simple statements will insure the company's growth as well as our own.

It suddenly dawned on me that every employee I had met really seemed to believe and live out that mission statement. They seemed proud to have it up front and public, right there in the elevator where guests could see it.

That experience has prompted a number of questions I ask when I work with governing boards. I begin with, "Where's your brass plaque?" and add, "Is your mission statement concise enough to fit on a plaque? Is it displayed prominently for all to see?" Other questions follow: "When was it written?" "Who owns it today?" "Do people believe it?" "How is it used (by staff, executive leadership, the board, and those the organization serves)?"

A mission statement is the *credo* (the "I believe" profession) of the Corporate Person. I've seen it printed at the head of the agenda for board meetings and on the back side of each member's tabletop nameplate—the side the member looks at during the meeting. I've heard the mission statement read aloud as meetings open and I know board members who have it committed to memory.

A 1989 Independent Sector report on effectiveness in not-for-profit organizations referred to a National Assembly study of successful leaders. The study reports:

> Belief in mission is one of the key factors that distinguishes the excellent leader from the run-of-the-mill. A board member commented, "He (the executive) believes in it—really believes in it. I think that is one of the characteristics you will find in anybody who works there. They all believe in it. It is an avocation as well as a vocation. I think that helps them too, because you can see it, you can feel it. It isn't a line of malarkey this guy is giving you; he believes it. You could see through that in a minute if it wasn't real."[6]

If that description is applicable to executive leadership, it most certainly ought also to be said of individual members of the board as they embody the Corporate Person that "They believe in their mission."

Several cautions need to be observed regarding mission statements. What the Corporate Person says it believes may look good on paper. However, words are one thing and actions may be something quite different. What belief statements need is the power to provide decision-making guidance. They need to be able to help the board steer away from diversions that are counterproductive to the declared mission.

The mission statement ought to be a bonding agent for the members of the board. They may not agree on everything. Indeed, they ought not to agree on everything, but one thing they must have in common as a unifying factor is their agreement on mission. Today, that is the hallmark of board composition and structure in effective not-for-profit boards. It departs from the old association model in which every member was elected to represent some specific segment of the community or constituency. The corporate model of board membership today calls for the election of individuals who—while coming from diverse backgrounds—will nonetheless represent the best interests of the whole community through their common commitment to the mission of the organization.

Moreover, the mission statement needs to accurately reflect what is really going on in the organization. In *The Addictive Organization* there is this interesting comment: "The organization becomes the addictive substance for its employees when the employees become hooked on the promise of mission and choose not to look at how the system is really operating. The organization becomes an addictive substance when its actions are excused because it has a lofty mission."[7]

That observation points to the fact that a mission statement can never be taken for granted. It cannot be allowed to simply provide grandiose phrases that don't mesh with reality. The Corporate Person needs to do some soul searching on a regular basis, and this brings us to the matter of conscience—that aspect of the corporate soul that requires the Corporate Person to act with integrity.

At issue is corporate trustworthiness. An organization earns the trust of the public—as well as its staff—through the clarity of its vision and values, and the way it articulates and acts on its statement of mission. It ought to be a mandate of the corporate conscience to do that with excellence, and that means full commitment and involvement on the part of the board.

Corporate conscience

In 1972, Robert Greenleaf observed, "[There is] a growing disquiet . . . a small but nonetheless significant public recognition that trustees and directors of major institutions are largely honorary and ineffective. In other words, they are not seen as trustworthy. The mere presence of trustees, in the absence of the performance which their place and title implies, does not generate trust."[8] Those words were written before the debacle that caused the boards of Covenant House, the PTL television ministry, and United Way to fall out of public trust and into disrepute almost two decades later.

Corporate conscience mandates accountability on the part of the Corporate Person. In keeping with its mission and values, the board has a moral obligation to scrutinize its own work and oversee the work of the entire organization. A clear corporate conscience is able to stand the test of public scrutiny and accountability to community and constituents. For example, in not-for-profit organizations this means maintaining a common commitment to a continuing struggle with "mission and margin"; that is, understanding that a positive cash flow is necessary in order to be benevolent. The conscience issue is this: "In keeping with our mission and values, how much positive cash flow and how much benevolence?"

Corporate conscience also means the Corporate Person engages in an ongoing self-assessment in terms of social accountability and definition of its charitable purposes before the law, the Internal Revenue Service, and the public on whose behalf the Corporate Person acts.

Can the corporate conscience be blunted? Of course. Peter Bell, writing for the National Center for Nonprofit Boards, cites a number of reasons why boards fail to fulfill their public trust and lose a sense of accountability. Among the most common are:

- The board may lack time and quality attention on the part of its members.
- The board may be too narrow, ingrown, and self-serving, and not sufficiently open, diverse, and outward-looking.
- The board may be composed of prima donnas whose concerns are more egocentric than corporate.
- The lines of authority between board and staff may be confused.
- The board may discourage vigorous discussion about ideas that guide the organization and the evaluation of performance.[9]

Guarding against the presence of any of these public "trust busters" again calls for the Corporate Person to do some regular soul searching. One way to do that is through an annual accountability audit. The National Center for Nonprofit Boards suggests questions such as these:

- Do we maintain clear financial records?
- Do we have a code of ethics and a conflict of interest policy?
- Do we cooperate with the media to tell our story with accuracy and integrity?
- Do we have a diverse board?
- Do we publish an annual report with adequate and accurate information?
- Do we have clear policy statements with no gaps in the areas of equity, money, and morals?
- Are we monitoring executive compensation with procedures that can be publicly defended?
- Are our actions congruent with our statement of mission?

Those questions all involve matters of conscience and can only be answered with integrity when the governance of the board is mission driven, grounded in values, and inspired by vision.

Questions for discussion
Chapter 3: Soul

1. **In not-for-profit governing boards . . . the bonding power of a common vision is absolutely essential. (p. 17)**

   A. What words describe the power of a common vision shared by the board on which you serve?

   B. What process does your board use for reviewing and projecting that vision?

   C. How much time at board meetings is spent looking ahead, with a vision for the future of your organization, in comparison to the time spent reviewing reports of work already accomplished?

   D. In what way has your board marked progress toward a goal, or celebrated an accomplishment? What did it feel like?

2. **Values statements are the moral fiber and spiritual strength of the Corporate Person. (p. 19)**

   A. What are the value words that describe the corporate soul of your board?

3. **The mission statement . . . needs to go to the heart of the organization's values and focus on its clear vision. (p. 20)**

   A. In what ways does the mission statement of your organization convey a passion that motivates both board and staff?

   B. When was the mission statement written, and by whom?

   C. Is your mission statement memorable?

4. **Corporate conscience mandates accountability on the part of the Corporate Person. (p. 22)**

   A. To whom is your board accountable? What steps does your board take to fulfill its public trust and demonstrate its accountability?

4 Mind

*Effective leaders never say I. They don't think I. They think we. They think team.
They take responsibility to make the team function, but the team gets the credit.
There is an identification with the task and with the group.
This is what creates trust and gets the task done.*

Peter Drucker

Thinking, deciding, remembering, learning—an individual's mind functions in those ways. So does the mind of the Corporate Person. Just as all boards of not-for-profit organizations do not function alike, the mind of the Corporate Person is as distinct and unique as the mind of each individual human being.

At the same time, while every board sees its environment, opportunities, and challenges from its own perspective and world view, the corporate mind has an added dimension. It must function collectively. The personified mind of the corporation brings together the brains, emotions, perceptions, biases, energy, and relative wisdom of a collection of volunteers. Since these individuals often represent a broad range of backgrounds and experience, this gathering has the potential for chaos and corporate schizophrenia. Fortunately, it also has the potential for creative thinking and decision making beyond the range of any single person's mind.

CREATING SYNERGY AND TRUST

Stephen Covey, in his book *The Seven Habits of Highly Effective People*, identifies the sixth habit as synergy—that is, a spirit of cooperation or teamwork where the whole is greater than the sum of its parts. Synergy, says Covey, results from valuing differences by bringing different perspectives together in the spirit of respectful communication. In such a setting, people feel free to seek the best possible alternative, and it is often the "third alternative," one that is substantially different from, and better than, the ideas originally proposed.[1]

For synergy to be effective, members of a board must understand that uniformity is not the same as unity, nor is sameness a synonym for oneness. The corporate mind recognizes the complementary nature of collective thinking that brings together a variety of cultures, traditions, opinions, and perspectives; a variety that provides the intellectual power center of the corporation. However, the synergistic ideal only works when there is conscious effort on the part of individual board members to make it work. John Carver writes, "As a board member, you are an unseverable part of a group transaction . . . so acting only through a group dynamic takes an extra measure of devotion and thought."[2]

The basic principle of both corporate body and corporate mind is "Without the board, you're not the board." The board member who insists on autonomous thinking, whose mind is made up before the meeting begins, and who is neither willing nor able to hear or appreciate the thinking of others, cannot effectively be part of the corporate mind. However, this doesn't mean that there can't be disagreement, dissent, or challenges to each other or to staff leaders in the course of corporate thinking. On the contrary, boards need enthusiasm for dissent "without being held hostage by dissenters."[3] At the same time, board members need to know that to think corporately means that while they may get their say, they may not always get their way.

Collective thinking is driven by a common purpose, a shared mission, and a commitment to work together for the common good of the organization. It's what Max De Pree refers to as a "covenantal relationship" that tolerates risk, forgives errors, and promotes active participation.[4] Board members are motivated to think corporately by clear vision (not tedious tasks), by a sense of momentum (not simply maintenance thinking), and by achieving goals (rather than continual muddling). Vision, momentum, and realized goals happen as board members put their minds together through board and board committee meetings.

Board meetings are literally "meetings of the mind," and each board meeting is the personification of the corporate mind because it:
- defines the collective identity of the group.
- creates a pool of shared knowledge.
- affirms a collective mission and individual contributions to that mission.
- promotes a common commitment to decision making and goal achievement.[5]

Board meetings define the wisdom, spirit, and soul of the Corporate Person as members deliberate, debate, decide, and determine the future of the organization. In his definitive monograph, "How to Run A Meeting," Antony Jay writes:

> In the simplest and most basic way, a meeting defines the team, the group, the unit. Those present belong to it; those absent do not. Everyone is able to look around and perceive the whole group and sense the collective

identity of which he or she forms a part. . . . A meeting is the place where the group revises, updates, and adds to what it knows as a group. Every group creates its own pool of shared knowledge, experience, judgment, and folklore. But the pool consists only of what the individuals have experienced or discussed as a group—i.e., those things that every individual knows that all the others know too. . . .

Some ethologists call this capacity to share knowledge and experience among a group "the social mind," conceiving it as a single mind dispersed among a number of skulls. . . .

A meeting helps every individual understand . . . the collective aim of the group. . . . A meeting is very often the only occasion where the team or group actually exists.[6]

How the corporate mind thinks in meetings depends greatly on two factors: how much board members trust each other and their staff, and the quality of information the staff provides. Trust is an elusive thing. When it exists in the corporate mind, it makes everything function smoothly. When it is lost or broken, it is almost impossible to repair.

Rather than attempting to rebuild trust after it breaks down, boards need to be proactive in establishing it. Among and between board members and executive staff, certain trust-building principles apply:

- Make efforts to know others, both board and executive staff, on a personal level outside the formal meetings of the board.
- Maintain appropriate communication among board members and executive staff on matters of mutual concern and for information sharing between meetings.[7]
- Do as much listening as talking.
- Affirm the skills and accomplishments of other board members and executive staff, and respect advice and opinions offered—even when you must respectfully disagree.
- Give executive staff and other board members the same level of professional courtesy and trust you expect from them.
- Keep a sense of humor in board work—lighten up and share some fun together!
- Encourage candid, accurate information—both good news and bad news, with recommendations and options from executive staff.
- Expect straightforward, honest disagreement and the challenging of ideas and opinions around the board table.
- Be dependable.
- Respect confidentiality.

Assuring good information

The effort to establish an atmosphere of mutual trust is essential for a healthy corporate mind and a key to effective meetings. But corporate thinking requires good information as well as good feelings. The board is legally and morally responsible for the success or failure of the organization. While it can delegate authority to executive staff for day-to-day operations, it cannot delegate ultimate responsibility for the organization. Ultimate decision making has to be done by the corporate mind, and the ability to do that depends upon it receiving good information.

The corporate mind needs to be constantly asking questions. In the interaction between board and executive staff, the role of board members is to probe and seek clarity, not to pontificate and pose as technical experts. The primary role of board members is to be question-askers, not answer-givers. Ultimately and collectively, board members must make decisions based on the information gathered through that questioning.

To ask the right questions and make sound decisions, the corporate mind must depend on the organization's executive staff to be the primary source and organizer of information into manageable parts and pieces. Problems arise when staff are guilty of providing information overload, drowning their boards in everything from unintelligibly complex strategic plans, to financial reports with pages of numbers and program details with endless bits of minutiae. Consequently, some boards become absolutely mind-boggled at just such times when the Corporate Person's mind needs to grasp the big picture, the overview, the helpful and decision-relevant information needed to think and act responsibly.

What should the board expect in terms of how information is shared and reported? There are three easily remembered rules for information gathering:

1. No surprises. The corporate mind should always be thinking "future." It needs to anticipate problems and be kept updated on plans and strategies. That means board members need to have adequate information prior to board meetings, including an agenda prepared in advance, written reports, realistic assessments of issues, and proposed options and alternative courses of action.

2. Don't pool ignorance. Peter Drucker writes about "organizing ignorance"[8]—that is, identifying what is not known or understood so that problems can be defined and information gathered before action is taken. The corporate mind cannot think or decide in a vacuum. It needs to deal with difficult situations and problems by weighing alternative solutions. It has a right to expect options to be presented by those who have expertise and technical understanding of the situation, and the primary source of that information is usually the executive staff.

3. Don't panic—think straight. Boards don't always react well to bad news, and executives don't relish the idea of sharing negative information. (Board developer Dan Cain tells of one administrator who described bringing bad news to his board as "bleeding in a pool of sharks.") With a lot of ego and reputation protection involved, it may be a natural inclination to gloss over or minimize problems. However, the corporate mind needs to know the straight facts—the bad news as well as the good news. Because the Corporate Person is ultimately responsible, this is where trust surfaces—among board members and between the board and the executive staff. Mistakes must not be concealed. Constructive criticism and corrective action must be offered and gracefully accepted. Hard questions must be asked, but not in ways that create embarrassment and defensive reactions. The goal of the corporate mind is to think clearly and collaboratively for the good of the organization and its mission. And in the process, the corporate mind makes decisions.

Consensus and decision making

How does the Corporate Person decide? The democratic process usually calls for debate, vote, and majority decision. In this way the corporation legally demonstrates in its minutes how decisions have been made, particularly where financial transactions and business decisions are involved. But in the process of arriving at decisions formally recorded with a vote, the thought process of the corporate mind is to work toward consensus, not toward a "house divided."

Glenn Tecker describes the corporate mind at work: "People can't make good decisions alone anymore. Things are too complex. Decisions need to be made by consensus. There can be disagreement without being disagreeable. Consensus is arrived at when no one in the group disagrees so strongly that they won't go along with the group's majority opinion."[9] Os Guinness observes that in dysfunctional groups "discussion is characterized by an unholy trio of insistent demands, unreconcilable differences, and inter-minable debates, all of which are 'unsettlable,'" whereas consensus is a matter of commitment to common ideals as well as compromise over competing interests.[10]

The very nature of corporate-mind decision making requires participation on the part of all board members, assisted by the executive staff and other resource people. Committees are useful in participatory thinking. However, their decision-making power is limited by the extent to which they are given decision-making authority. Their primary role is to develop and describe alternative solutions for the board to approve or send back for additional development. The value of committees, task forces, or other subgroups is that they involve more people in the corporate thought process. They solicit input and provide feedback regarding options and alternatives, and they help build consensus.

Sometimes decisions are made with difficulty and one expects that a variety of opinions and ideas will be offered and tested. Resistance and dissent are to be expected but, as Antony Jay observes, "real opposition to decisions within organizations usually consists of one part disagreement with the decision to nine parts resentment at not being consulted before the decision."[11] While at times there will be conflict, full participation of all board members in thinking through issues—well in advance of the time decisions must be made—strengthens the corporate mind. That means pulling together the thinking of both the dominant and more submissive members of the board. If everyone is committed to working toward consensus, dealing with conflicting opinions and hard questions toughens and trains the mental processes.

Some additional observations on decision making are useful:

1. Clear vision is a valuable point of reference when making hard choices. All board members and executive staff should agree that the mission and goals of the organization must not be compromised.

2. Patience is a virtue. The corporate mind needs to be reminded that it should not jump to quick conclusions. The rule of thumb is that reversible decisions can be made quickly, but nearly irreversible decisions must take more time and thought.

3. Assumptions need to be tested. Worst-case scenarios need to be looked at honestly. The issue or problem needs to be defined. The board needs to agree on preferred outcomes and strategies for bridging the gap between the problem and proposed solutions. It is not uncommon for the corporate mind to be subjected to mental fatigue because this all takes time, but the process is often a real test of the Corporate Person's commitment.

4. There comes a time for a decision, a time when discussion and debate must cease. Decisive leadership is evidenced not only by individuals but by the

Corporate Person. However, the board must understand that when it decides, it is a collective decision. Not everyone may be pleased with the outcome, but that must not deter the decision-making process.

5. Once a decision has been reached, it is the position of the Corporate Person. That is an essential fact and must be understood. Membership on the board obligates members to support decisions and accept accountability for their results. Andrew Swanson put it succinctly: "Individual board members must support the decisions of the full board in public even if they disagreed with those decisions when they were made. Part of being a mature person is recognition of the fact that one's opinions are not always shared by one's peers. Should you feel strongly enough about an issue, then you must leave the board and work for change from the outside. Publicly divided boards do not gladden the hearts of the agency's clients and are poor candidates for philanthropy."[12]

Corporate decision making is also made more complex by the issues of conflicting loyalties and duality. The corporate mind is radically affected by the participation of board members with divided loyalties, hidden agendas, the potential for personal gain, or the influence of nepotism. While it may never be completely possible to assemble a group of board members without some vested interests and deep personal commitments, the Corporate Person needs to know what those are. That is done by an annual process of disclosure, and by clear policies for dealing with conflicts of interest. It is information for the corporate memory, and that brings us to another aspect of the corporate mind.

PRESERVING THE CORPORATE MEMORY

Some say that institutional memory is the shortest memory of all. If it is not recorded, it lasts only as long as recollections in the minds of individuals and even then, those recollections may vary greatly from one person to another. Long-term board members often carry with them historical memory of the organization. They have a sense of why the organization began, together with its original mission and motivation. However, that memory disappears when they leave the board. That's why written mission statements, values, and principles need to be preserved along with a recorded history of the organization.

Without historical memory, the culture of an organization—its traditions, beliefs, and the inspiration of its founders—cannot be understood or appreciated. Significantly, when an organization forgets the passion and commitment out of which it began, it risks jeopardizing its future. A little allegory illustrates this point:

> A spider set out to spin a web high in the recesses of an old barn. He began with a single filament attached to a rafter, dropping down to a beam, then swinging back and forth in the dusty darkness. For days he labored, carefully spinning an intricate network of silken strands. Occasionally a shaft of sunlight would shine through a crevice, highlighting the beauty of the web.
>
> Finally, it was completed, and the spider settled down in its center, content to admire its construction and bask in the comfort of what he had created. As the spider looked at his masterpiece, he noticed one seemingly irrelevant thread, rising up into the darkness to the rafters near the roof. "I can't remember where that came from," he thought to himself. Reaching up with a claw, he grabbed that slender strand. Tugging and pulling, he broke it loose from the moorings where it had been anchored long ago, and the entire web collapsed around him.

As new members join a board and enter into the corporate mind, their orientation ought to include the history of the organization. In this way they know about its inception and growth, and the landmark events that have influenced its current mission and status. Some organizations have developed a time-line chart as an orientation visual aid to graphically illustrate dates, people, and events in their histories. Board developer Stuart Entz points out that awareness of the past "is consistent with the corporate concept of a continuous, immortal person [the Corporate Person]. Certainly current affairs of the corporation flow from and must be viewed in their historic perspective."[13]

Corporate memory does not only relate to organizational history. It also relates to matters as current as the last board meeting or the information shared during a meeting in progress. Karl Mathiasen III observes, "It's a funny thing, but boards . . . generally have no memory worth mentioning. Staffs are so preoccupied with their work that they are continually surprised by a board that seems to have irresponsible lapses of memory. Exasperating as it may be for staffs, it is a fact of life that volunteer, very part-time boards . . . do not remember well what happened at the last meeting, much less what they agreed to do several months ago. . . . Staffs think that their boards 'must' know more and do more than they will actually know or do. Staffs are offended by boards that doze and doodle during long reports and endless agendas, but the fact is that boards can only be expected to absorb and digest so much information and to conduct so much business . . . board members are busy people, they have short attention spans, and resent the pressure of endless agendas."[14]

Mathiasen's comments may seem to be too much of a caricature for the many not-for-profit boards that take their responsibilities with a high degree of commitment. Nevertheless, every board's corporate memory is assisted by some practical steps.

1. The first of these is *board policy development.* A functional definition of policy is: *basic, established, written courses of action.*

"Basic" describes the nature of policy. It deals with the essential rules by which the board conducts itself and the limits within which the executive works. "Established" refers to the fact that policy is a product of the corporate mind, having been developed and voted on by the board. "Written" means decisions are recorded and preserved, not only in the organization's minutes but also compiled in a board policy handbook. Written policies are essential to preserving the corporate memory, both for long-term and incoming members. The latter will discover that a compilation of written policies is an invaluable part of an orientation manual.

In the corporate mind, written policy is vital because it establishes a common understanding and promotes consistent action over a period of time. Because the corporate memory has been sustained, it minimizes redeliberating issues.

2. Another step in preserving corporate memory is the use of an *annotated agenda.* This includes the list of items to be dealt with in meetings, descriptions of issues, and proposed motions to be brought before the board, and the major assumptions that underlie those alternatives and proposals.

In a financial agenda, information on benchmark ratios and percentages established by board policy for measuring trends and analyzing growth need to be included in order to refresh the corporate memory. Including this information in an annotated agenda requires adequate advance preparation by executive staff, committees, and the board chair prior to meetings.

3. Carefully writing and recording *meeting minutes* is a third essential step in preserving the corporate memory. Minutes preserve decisions made, policies developed, and a record of the organization's adherence to its mission and legal responsibilities. They reflect the participation of board members by listing those present and those absent. By reading and approving them at subsequent board meetings, they provide opportunity for review and correction of past actions. Finally, they provide—in verbatim resolutions—specific actions enacted by the board, all for the purpose of preserving corporate memory.

4. One final helpful step to aid the memory of the corporate mind is to *develop an organizational calendar.* Bringing a group of volunteer board

members together on a regular basis requires their priority time commitment. To agree well in advance on a regular schedule of meetings—as well as special events—is both a courtesy and a discipline that keeps the Corporate Person on track.

CORPORATE LEARNING

Out of that discipline the corporate mind thinks, decides, remembers, and engages in a continual learning process. The Corporate Person learns from a variety of sources including presentations from staff; briefings from executive leaders; and through reading, consultations, and conferences. Most of all, members of the Corporate Person learn from each other. It's a dynamic Peter Senge calls "team learning":

> The discipline of team learning involves mastering the practices of dialogue and discussion, the two distinct ways that teams converse. In dialogue, there is the free and creative exploration of complex and subtle issues, a deep "listening" to one another and suspending one's own views. By contrast, in discussion different views are presented and defended and there is a search for the best view to support decisions that must be made. . . .
> . . . the discipline of team learning, like any discipline, requires practice. . . . Imagine trying to build a great theater ensemble or a great symphony orchestra without rehearsal. Imagine a championship sports team without practice. In fact, the process whereby such teams learn is through continual movement between practice and performance, practice, performance, practice again, perform again.[15]

For the Corporate Person, learning together as a board—a discipline of the corporate mind—happens most regularly in the work of planning. It's a regular routine of practice and performance, looking toward the future, studying internal and external forces and environments, and examining strengths and weaknesses. It involves developing goals, objectives, and strategies. It means writing plans and then monitoring, evaluating, and correcting them while projecting the future.

All of this is corporate learning; plans are the product of the corporate mind, and learning the answers to two questions is the essence of planning. The questions are "Are we planning to do the right things?" and "Are we planning to do things the right way?" Boards have sometimes learned from hard experience that unless they deal adequately with the first question, the second question isn't worth asking. As organizational expert William Conrad has said, "The greatest sin in the world is to do something very well that should never have been done at all."

While corporate learning that comes from planning may often come through trial-and-error, midcourse corrections, and just plain muddling, corporate learning can also be done carefully, productively, and intelligently. The wisdom of the corporate mind—manifested in the synergy of corporate thinking, deciding, and remembering—produces a mature organization; one continually learning and growing into a stronger, more cohesive Corporate Person.

Questions for discussion
Chapter 4: Mind

1. **The corporate mind has an added dimension. It must function collectively. (p. 25)**

   A. Describe examples of teamwork and collective thinking in the board on which you serve. Do board members think and speak more in "I" language or "we" language?

   B. How does your board demonstrate the difference between unity and uniformity? To what extent are diverse points of view respected in an atmosphere of trust?

2. **Board meetings are literally "meetings of the mind." (p. 26)**

   A. How does your board intentionally work to build trust among members, and between board and staff?

   B. To what extent is the information you receive before board meetings timely and adequate for collaborative decision making?

   C. How does your board fulfill its role as "hard question-askers?"

   D. Once decisions are made, how well are those decisions respected by board members as the will of the corporate mind?

3. **Some say that institutional memory is the shortest memory of all. (p. 31)**

   A. When was your organization's written history last shared with all members of your board? Who has the responsibility for preserving and updating that history?

   B. Where are the policies of your board recorded? What is the process for organizing and maintaining your board policy handbook?

   C. How soon after board meetings are the minutes distributed for review by the members of the board?

4. **The corporate mind thinks, decides, remembers, and engages in a continual learning process. (p. 34)**

   A. What has your board learned lately? What would be helpful to enhance that learning?

5 BEHAVIOR

Would you rather work as part of an outstanding group or be part of a group of outstanding individuals?

Max De Pree

Here's a little horror story to set the stage for some thoughts on the behavior of the Corporate Person.

Several decades ago, when the Great Society was in its ascendancy and federal funding for social programs was abundant, a community not-for-profit agency for teaching independent living skills to the developmentally disabled was organized in a small western city. It had a great altruistic mission and corporate soul.

The corporate body, its board, was composed of a doctor, a banker, a lawyer, a social worker, and a homemaker. All of them became involved because of their volunteer spirit, community concern, and compassion for the less fortunate. They all brought important skills to the formation of this Corporate Person. However, they were also very busy people involved in other things and their idealism did not carry with it a long-term commitment to the agency or its mission.

One thing was clear in their founding stage of corporate life: None of them had the time, resources, or skills to manage the agency's day-to-day activities. Therefore they hired an administrator—a well-meaning, likable fellow with a social service background who, unfortunately, had few skills in budgeting or managing staff. He hired a program director who was great at generating grants but less than adequate at fiscal management and cost control.

The board members, thinking that all was well, let their corporate mind fall asleep. They met occasionally, primarily for social functions and to hear glowing reports from their administrator about grants received, additional staff hired, and new programs generated. They asked few questions as they watched the agency budget grow from an original $300,000 to an annual income of $2,300,000. Much of that income was from state and federal contracts to serve not only the developmentally disabled but also elderly and low-income people. The mission and the culture of the organization had changed radically but the behavior of the board had not. They still enjoyed the social time at meetings, the community prestige of their association with distinguished colleagues, and a general sense of corporate well-being.

Until one evening when they were called together for an "emergency meeting" and told—to their shock and surprise—that *they* were terribly over-extended financially and in deep legal trouble; "they" meaning the agency, the board corporately, and even the individual board members.

The immediate crisis centered around a state government contract for $100,000 to distribute surplus commodity cheese to low-income families. The board had blithely approved the contract as it had approved so many before. Only after the contract was in place did the administrator discover it was going to take at least $120,000 to implement. He'd found, to his dismay, that the cheese didn't come in neat little pre-sliced packages. It came in bulk and needed to be cut. The special cutting equipment the agency purchased turned out to be too small because the cheese came in 300-pound barrels! Expenses piled up while the cash flow diminished. Specters of mismanagement and nonmanagement reared their ugly heads.

What the board heard at the emergency meeting for the first time was that there had been cash-flow problems over the past year. The administrator had been "temporarily coping" with these by not paying $42,000 of withholding taxes for 30 employees—a federal offense for which board members at that time could be held directly liable.[1]

In addition, the agency had borrowed $121,000 in unsecured notes from a local bank. That decision had been made unilaterally by the administrator and the board member who happened to be the bank loan officer. Now the bank was pressing for immediate repayment. However, the agency and the bank found their predicament compounded by the fact that the agency's attorney board member was also the bank's attorney and he had known nothing about the loans! To add to the legal entanglements, the social worker on the board was an employee of the state Department of Public Assistance, which was threatening legal action for nonperformance on the cheese distribution contract. Furthermore, the Internal Revenue Service loomed over this Corporate Person and the individual board members for nonpayment of withholding taxes.

At this point, the board's corporate mind lost its collective wits and panicked. The board fired the administrator and board members assumed the management responsibilities themselves. To cut costs, they also terminated the program director and reduced staff positions they could no longer afford. That resulted in contracted programs and services being curtailed and even less income production.

The agency ground to a halt in a matter of months but the liability of the board members did not. The state had incorporated this body with a purpose for existence and trusted it with a fiduciary obligation. It began an inquiry, demanding continuing accountability and ultimate responsibility from the board. The results were sleepless nights and worried days for the board members.

The story has a "good news-bad news" ending. After a lengthy investigation, the board was cleared of criminal misconduct charges and misappropriation of funds. While a state audit concluded that too many financial records were missing to bring charges, it also concluded that "massive overspending and mismanagement" had led to the downfall of the organization. This still left the corporation liable to civil suits.

Four months later, board members received registered letters directing them individually to remit $33,000 as their share of the legal obligation for which they were being held personally liable. Counter suits followed and repercussion in the community continued long afterward.

As extreme as it may seem, that's the kind of story that sends board members scrambling for reassurance that their directors' and officers' insurance policies are in place! It also gives potential board members pause about volunteering their service to not-for-profit organizations in their communities.

Are the risks too great? The answer depends on the behavior of the Corporate Person—its culture, accountability, trust relationships, and its ultimate assumption of responsibility.

BEHAVIOR AND CORPORATE CULTURE

Every not-for-profit board has a personality that makes its Corporate Person as distinctive as individual human beings are from one another. A board's "culture" may be defined as "its collective personality and style of governing, based on perception of its role, understanding of its functions, and ownership of its mission, all of which is demonstrated in its corporate behavior."

To prevent the schizophrenic behavior of the board described in the horror story, the focus of a board's culture must be on the word *corporate*. Collective activity—driven by a clear vision, strong commitment, mutual responsibility, and open communication—is fundamental. The question boards need to answer is "*How* do we do *what* we do *together*?"

Professor Larry Lauer of Texas Christian University points out that "an organization's culture really begins with its founding. It relates to what the founders proposed to do and how they set out to do it. Fulfilling that dream, realizing that vision, and establishing appropriate behaviors . . . are critically important." Lauer explains that "Culture establishes how things are done and what beliefs cannot be compromised. Cultural traits provide the bonding that brings people together and establishes their collective identity. . . . Strong organizations have strong cultures."[2]

That is not to say that board behavior doesn't change over time. Boards who are locked into a monolithic "we've always done it this way" mind-set may be able to establish a collective identity, but they are going to have great difficulty coping with change. And change is the name of the game as term limits and rotation of board members bring new individuals into the corporate body. How do they learn the behavior of the board? How is the culture to be appropriated?

A great many board members spend the first year or more of their tenure simply trying to figure out what is going on, while more experienced members do the discussing, deliberating, and deciding. Breaking into the established culture isn't easy unless there is an intentional effort to make it happen. One of the simplest and most direct methods used by a growing number of boards is the "buddy system" that pairs experienced members with new board members for the first year. As a part of new-member orientation, this pairing permits and encourages peer conversation and reflection on what's happening. The culture becomes infectious and, assuming it includes a healthy set of behaviors, it can draw new members into a corporate identity with increased confidence, participation, awareness, and commitment to vision and mission.

Pluralism and diversity

The great challenge to the Corporate Person's behavior is that members join a board as individuals. It is not always easy for individuals who are accustomed to leading and making decisions on their own to behave, think, or speak corporately. For example, it has been observed that board members "are often drawn from the ranks of corporate executives, senior partners in a professional practice, or other positions at or near the top of an organizational hierarchy. In these roles, they customarily have considerable individual authority to act and thus play a more directive role in decision making. Trustees, by comparison, are peers. Each trustee's vote carries equal weight in board decisions and individual trustees rarely have any authority to act formally and independently on the board's behalf."[3] In a nation where individualism, pluralism, and autonomy are highly valued, working as a collaborative team is sometimes an unfamiliar experience. For board members to develop a collective identity as one "corporate" person in the eyes of the law can be difficult. However, understanding the importance of that identity is critical to the life of the organization the board governs because it determines the board's behavior.

Pluralism is a reality in our society. Defined as "a state in which members of diverse groups maintain an autonomous participation in and development of their culture or special interest," it describes the milieu from which board members are drawn. Yet, when they are brought into a corporate culture, there is the implicit expectation that they will share some mutual mission and similar values to work for the common good of the organization they have been chosen to govern. John Gardner has said it well:

> A society in which pluralism is not undergirded by some shared values and held together by some measure of mutual trust simply cannot survive. Pluralism that reflects no commitments whatever to the common good is pluralism gone berserk. A primary task of our dispersed leadership is to achieve a workable level of unity within the society. It is well to specify a workable level because the last thing we want is unqualified or oppressive unity.... Unfortunately, a high proportion of leaders in all segments of our society today—business, labor, the professions, and so on—are rewarded for single-minded pursuit of the interests of their group. They are rewarded for doing battle, not compromising.[4]

Gardner's comments about "a workable level of unity" need to be underlined. Corporate behavior should in no way require all board members to think, speak, or look alike. Diversity in the Corporate Person is to be valued and encouraged, but diversity should not carry with it battleground implications.

Theologian Patricia Dutcher-Walls emphasized that theme when she said, "Taking diversity and pluralism seriously means a clear and consistent policy of inclusiveness, of recruiting ... and supporting people from the diverse ... backgrounds that make up the wider ... community. For all the groups involved, it means becoming an ally with groups other than one's own—taking their agenda to heart, asking how people can work together, and being willing to do the work. It means, finally, being willing to be changed by the inclusiveness one believes in."[5] When that attitude becomes part of an organization's culture, the behavior of the Corporate Person is shaped and changed for the better.

Nevertheless, the board is still made up of individuals with special gifts and abilities and each has unique personality quirks and flaws as well. Does the variety contribute to constructive activity and healthy governance, or does it do violence to the nature of the Corporate Person? Max De Pree offers a model from the corporate culture of his organization:

> When we think of *corporate* diversity, we think about the gifts and talents and commitment that each of us as individuals bring to the group effort. Channeled correctly and integrated properly, our diversity can be our greatest strength. But there is always the temptation to use these gifts for our personal benefit rather than dedicating them to the best interest of the group. If used selfishly, they will cause serious internal erosion. The process of integration is simply abandoning oneself to the strengths of others, being vulnerable to what others can do better than we can.[6]

There are three standards by which the behavior of the Corporate Person are defined:

1. Relationships of trust
2. Accountability
3. The principle of delegated authority/retained responsibility

When these standards are unshakable elements of the board's culture, board behavior will be above reproach and disasters like the one described in the horror story at the beginning of this chapter will be averted.

Relationships of trust

In incorporating an organization, the state gives the organization its legal existence as a Corporate Person. With that charter of incorporation, the state entrusts that person with a "fiduciary responsibility;" that is, a trust obligation to act "in good faith" from which comes the commonly used title, "board of trustees."[7]

Regardless of whether a board refers to itself as *trustees* or *directors*—titles used almost interchangeably in common parlance—or some other title such as *governors* or *regents*, the trust obligation is paramount. To clarify that role in terms of corporate behavior, periodically the board ought to reflect on two simple questions:

1. Who trusts us?
2. With what have we been entrusted?

The answer to the first question requires a listing of *stake*holders (as opposed to *stock*holders in for-profit corporations). When done carefully and comprehensively, that listing should produce a rather formidable roster. It will include people and organizations who have a stake in the behavior and decisions of the board, depend on the board's leadership, and hold the board in a position of trust. This concept is further developed in the next section on accountability.

The answer to the second question, "With what have we been entrusted?" has several dimensions. The classic description of the board's trust obligation has been defined in terms of three duties: obedience, loyalty, and care.

The duty of obedience is the fundamental obligation implied in incorporation: to govern within the limitations of the law, the regulations imposed by the legal codes and rules, and in compliance with the policies and governing documents of the organization. A basic tenet of the *duty of obedience* that is abused by some board members, and misunderstood by many others, is the adage "Without the board, you're not the board." A member who assumes authority not granted by the board, or acts outside board meetings as though he or she were "the board," violates the concept of the Corporate Person and is disobedient to the limitations placed on board membership. Before the law, the board exists as a collective body under obligation to do only what is described in the corporation's articles of incorporation and in the state's statutes regarding not-for-profit corporations.

The duty of loyalty is essentially the responsibility of the board to act in good faith. Loyalty to the organization, its mission, and its purpose must take precedence over any individual board member's self-interest or loyalty to certain individuals or groups. The board is obligated to see that the organization it governs is managed honestly, without willful or fraudulent breaches of the trust relationship. This is where conflicts of interest and duality (divided loyalties) emerge. Potential conflicts of interest always exist in the boards of organizations. That fact is neither unavoidable, nor necessarily undesirable. Individuals who serve on boards are active, involved, influential people who are elected because of their interest, familiarity, skills, professional experience, and connections. In some cases, they may be insiders in terms of their involvement in and knowledge of the organization.

The issue is how the board deals with conflicts and divided loyalties. There are obvious conflicting behaviors such as taking advantage of opportunities to make money off the organization while ostensibly serving as an uncompensated volunteer member of the board. There are also issues of divided loyalty that go beyond financial gain. The corporate life of the board can be severely threatened by nepotism, vested personal interests that affect objective decision making, preferential treatment, and favoritism. Breaches of confidentiality, provincial and personal biases that border on narrow-mindedness, misuse of status and authority, and a host of other behaviors produce divided loyalties. The integrity of the Corporate Person is tested by these situations.

While policies and procedures for disclosure of potential conflicts may be in place, it is ultimately the collective will and a culture of trustworthiness that determines how the Corporate Person behaves. The matter of conscience becomes apparent in the need for board members to maintain balance and objectivity when conflicts and dual loyalties emerge. Their willingness to understand and follow policy, both individually and collectively, is a trust responsibility that reflects the integrity of the board as a whole.

The duty of care is the obligation of the board to see that the organization is managed with prudent business judgment. With a not-for-profit corporation, the standard of prudent business judgment—"How would you manage your own business if it were of a similar magnitude?"—may differ from a proprietary business. Viewed in the light of purpose and mission statements of the organization, the determinative question for the Corporate Person is "What would a reasonable and prudent person decide in terms of the stated purposes, policies, and mission of this organization?" In other words, the behavior dictated by the *duty of care* for the Corporate Person is not simply protection of assets, but preservation of mission.

What this obviously requires of the entire board is participatory behavior that is diligent, attentive, and informed about the business and mission of the organization.

Specifically, corporate behavior requires:
- consistent attendance at board meetings.[8]
- care in the appointment of executive leadership authorized to manage the organization.
- ongoing supervision of employees through that executive leadership.
- attention to the business affairs, finances, and records of the organization.
- avoidance of mismanagement/the failure to manage adequately. Mismanagement may take the form of accepting uncritically and without question any action of the board or recommendation of staff, thus knowingly allowing illegal activities and transactions; decision making apart from legally called meetings; and ignoring legal requirements, governing documents, and board policy.
- avoidance of nonmanagement/the failure to manage at all (such as nonattendance at meetings and ignorance of corporate operations and activities).

For a case study in bad board behavior and the duties of care, loyalty, and obedience, reflect on the horror story at the beginning of this chapter.

There is another, less often defined, dimension to relationships of trust and the Corporate Person's fiduciary responsibility. Robert Greenleaf described it this way: "It is . . . the obligation of trustees to fulfill what their title implies and become initiating builders of trust. They should see this as their role."[9]

To be "builders of trust" requires that board members collectively have credibility and integrity in the community and among the constituents they serve, in both individual and corporate behavior. It also means that board members will work at building trust among themselves. Equally important, board members as "builders of trust" will work to develop a collaborative, respectful trust relationship with their executive leader. That requires mutual effort and accountability.

Trust building is challenged by many less than desirable behaviors that threaten the Corporate Person's ability to function. There are negative personal characteristics that can be attributed to some board and staff members. The adjectives are many: maverick, dysfunctional, recalcitrant, adversarial, obnoxious. If those personality traits tend to break down trust, they become malignant and corrosive in the corporate body. Many potentially good trust relationships have fallen victim to bad personal chemistry.

On the other hand, trust can be enabled and affirmed even in difficult relationships (see chapter 4 for specific positive trust-building techniques). For the Corporate Person to meet a standard of trust, it must work to develop an atmosphere of trust among its members and the community it serves, as well as a mutual sense of trust with the staff it directs. To have trust means vitality; to lose it spells disaster.

ACCOUNTABILITY

The second standard by which the Corporate Person's behavior should be measured is accountability. If trust relationships describe the internal integrity of the Corporate Person, accountability focuses on its external relationships and behaviors.

Board members who trust each other will also hold each other accountable for behaving corporately, rather than autonomously. A major problem in corporate behavior surfaces when individual members do not respect the equal role and responsibility of other members in speaking, deliberation, and decision making. That includes such specific behavior as absenteeism, inattention, breaches of confidentiality, and other inappropriate activity. It also includes preventing equal access to information for all board members through over-zealous executive committees, rump-sessions of "insider" board members, and inappropriate communication between an executive and one or more board members in order to circumvent open discussion.

First and foremost, board members are accountable to each other. They owe each other a shared commitment to a common mission and a willingness to work constructively together to accomplish the organization's goals. There is an apocryphal story about an organization in a community where autonomy was so highly valued that the motto of the board was "every man for himself!" On the contrary, "Because the board's authority derives from its actions as a governing body, it must function as a cohesive team. There is little or no room on the board for the 'lone ranger' trustee."[10]

It is, however, a contradiction to say that a not-for-profit board is accountable only to itself. If the primary purpose of a not-for-profit organization is service to community, then no board governing such an organization ought to be self-serving. There is a huge array of people with a real stake in the outcomes of the organization who depend on the behavior of the Corporate Person, and who believe that Person will be accountable to them.

Who are these stakeholders? Think of them in terms of a ripple effect: concentric rings of accountability moving out from the board. First of all, there are the primary recipients of the organization's care or service. Then there are the:

- immediate and extended families of those service recipients.
- staff who deliver services and care.
- corporate members or sponsors who form the corporation and elect the board.
- communities in which the organization exists and from which it draws its clients and support.
- state, which grants incorporation (and may require regulation).
- funding sources, including donors, government entitlement/granting programs, and foundations.
- vendors who provide goods and support services.

All of these and more depend on the effective behavior of the board, and to each of them the board is accountable.

How does the Corporate Person meet the standard of accountability? There are many ways, beginning with the effort to identify and understand those stakeholders and their expectations. Then, as a corporate body, a number of attitudes and activities follow. They are:

- an annual report of the corporation to its stakeholders.
- an annual certified independent audit.
- filing of the Internal Revenue Service Form 990 as required by law for all not-for-profit organizations.[11]
- a clearly displayed statement of mission and other documents and symbols identifying the organization's purpose and culture.
- adoption of a statement of ethics and other written board policies relating to corporate accountability.
- accurate records, including financial reports, that meet accepted accounting standards and demonstrate the board's fiscal integrity.
- respect for inclusiveness and diversity that reflects the community in the makeup of the board.
- provision of just treatment and compensation of staff.
- recognition and encouragement of volunteers.
- ongoing communication with stakeholders that includes acknowledgments of support and interpretation of purpose and program to the public.
- a continuing commitment to public service that includes the ability to demonstrate charitable activity in and on behalf of the community.

All of the above reflect the personality and behavior of the Corporate Person displaying attitudes of service, self-confidence, humility, and integrity before the stakeholders to whom it is accountable.

Delegated authority/retained responsibility

If the first two standards for defining the behavior of the Corporate Person, *trust* and *accountability*, are somewhat intangible and philosophical, the third definition is clearly pragmatic. The principle of *delegated authority/retained responsibility* deals with the roles and relationship of board and staff. Practiced diligently, this principle enables the Corporate Person to "mind its own business"; that is, the business of governing, giving direction, dealing with the big picture, and assuring the organization is well-managed.

It begins with an understanding of corporate power. "Trustees have a kind of power that administrators and staffs do not have—they have the legal power to manage everything in the institution; they have all the legal power there is. They may delegate some of it, but they can also take it back. *They cannot give any of it away irretrievably and still be trustees.* . . . This is the central issue of trusteeship: trustees hold ultimate power but they do not use it operationally. Yet they are responsible for its use."[12] In short, the principle is: "You can delegate authority. You cannot delegate responsibility."

Having said that, it is important to emphasize that "responsibility for everything doesn't mean the board does everything."[13] There is a fine balance, a creative tension, that exists in the way board and staff function as a collaborative team. On the one hand, much has been written about micromanaging, the tendency to "pull up the flowers to see if the roots are growing" as it was once defined by board developer V. Clayton Sherman.[14] On the other hand, there is the equally destructive behavior of macromanaging, the inclination to get so far removed from operational management that, when it ought to be asserting its power and responsibility, the board shows little awareness or involvement.

The reality is that boards and staff both abhor vacuums of leadership. If a board is inept or ineffective, a strong executive leader will step in and do what must be done to keep the organization going. However, if a weak executive invites or allows the board to overstep its appropriate boundaries, that board will likely get into the organization's daily operations. While that tendency to fill a leadership void may be seen as being responsible, or "keeping things under control," what may seem a necessary temporary correction may become a permanent part of organizational culture. The strong executive may decide it's easier to keep the board controlled by continuing to do its thinking for them. The board with weak executive leadership may develop the habit of attempting to do the operational management, problem-solving, and supervision it ought to have delegated and expected that executive to do, thereby attempting to exert control in ways that it has neither the time nor the skills to do. In both cases, the potential for organizational chaos is increased, not diminished. (See the horror story at the beginning of this chapter.)

Margaret Wheatley, in her remarkable book, *Leadership and the New Science*, uses quantum physics and chaos theory to give new insights into the way organizations function—or ought to function. A couple of her observations are relevant here: "All this time we have created trouble for ourselves in organizations by confusing control with order. . . . If organizations are machines, control makes sense. If organizations are process structures, then seeking to impose control through permanent structure is suicide. If we believe that acting responsibly means exerting control by having our hands into everything, then we cannot hope for anything except what we already have—a treadmill of effort and life-destroying stress."[15]

Wheatley continues: "If we succeed in maintaining focus, rather than hands-on control, we also create the flexibility and responsibleness that every organization craves. What leaders are called upon to do in a chaotic world is to shape their organizations through concepts, not through elaborate rules or structures."[16]

The idea of the Corporate Person is this kind of an organization-shaping concept. The corporate board is not a machine. It is a living, thinking, relation-building, collectively responsible *person*. In delegating authority, it demonstrates trust and expects accountability, and in the process it grows and matures, as do those with whom it collaborates to accomplish its goals.

Authorization is a key word for responsible board behavior. It applies primarily to authorization of executive leadership for operational management. The board does that by establishing policies that set upper limits beyond which executive decisions cannot be made without board approval. This type of authorization demonstrates considerable trust and latitude since it expects the executive to implement the board's goals and plans without constant supervision. Accountability is maintained through the board's regular monitoring of progress on goals and plans. That monitoring is the primary measure of executive performance and organizational accomplishment.[17]

However, delegating authority does not just apply to the board-executive relationship. The same principle applies to the activity of board committees and task forces. These are always limited by what their job descriptions authorize, and they are always accountable to the full board for their decisions and behavior. That principle is particularly tested and challenged at times by executive committees that preempt the responsibility of the full board by arbitrarily excluding them, withholding information, or taking action that is the full board's responsibility. Executive committees need to be reviewed on a regular basis by the board to see if they are exceeding the limits of their designated authority.

Delegation of authority with retained responsibility is a fundamental principle for the behavior of individual members of the board.[18] Violations of that principle run the gamut from presuming to speak for the board without board consent to attempting unilaterally to influence executive decision making. Examples include intimidation or criticism of staff while they are at work, making promises or negotiating for board contracts without knowledge of the board, and organizing "star-chamber" sessions of a select in-group of board members for special action.

Certain observations about *delegated authority/retained responsibility*, as they apply to individual members of the corporate body, are basic to good board behavior:

- The entire membership of the board, the Corporate Person, has a collective legal responsibility for the organization.

- Only the board as a body has the authority to govern.
- Without the board, no individual *is* the board.
- Board decisions must be made collectively, in legally called meetings of the board.
- Board members have no individual authority except that which has been given them by board authorization.
- Individually, board members have no authority to act unilaterally for the board, or to supervise staff without authorization.
- The strength and abilities of the board as a Corporate Person lie in the combined strength and ability of its members.
- A board member who makes decisions without engaging in board deliberation can both harm the organization's programs and jeopardize a personal reputation.
- Board members must respect corporate decision making by recognizing that once a decision is made it represents the will of the "corporate mind."

As in all aspects of the Corporate Person's life, the board demonstrates responsibility by holding its individual members accountable for behaving corporately.

A final word on corporate behavior: Earlier in this chapter we discussed the matter of culture, highlighting the positive aspects of diversity. We defined three fundamental standards—trust, accountability, and responsibility/authority—as positive behaviors. There is one other element that contributes to the Corporate Person's attitude and personality: a culture of gratitude.

There are many reasons why people serve on volunteer boards. Edward Lindeman has a wonderful comment about a motivation that may not be understood as it ought to be:

> The act of volunteering is an assertion of individual worth. The person who, of his own free-will, decides to work for the good of the community is in effect saying: "I have gifts and talents that are needed. I am a person who accepts responsibility, not because it is imposed on me, but rather because I wish to be useful. My right to be thus used is a symbol of my personal dignity and worth.

On the one hand, nobody likes to be used (translate: "abused") when they volunteer. It makes for bad attitudes and bad behavior. On the other hand, it's a different story when a volunteer offers gifts and skills and says "use me." To care about a community, organization, or mission enough to offer a part of one's life is an expression of gratitude, an appreciation for the opportunity to share and serve.

It is life-affirming for the Corporate Person to take time now and then to reflect on the collective gifts and skills its members bring; then acknowledge them—not for individual ego-satisfaction, but simply to build up the "attitude of gratitude" that strengthens and transforms corporate behavior.

Questions for discussion
Chapter 5: Behavior

1. Every not-for-profit board has a personality that makes its Corporate Person as distinctive as individual human beings are from one another. (p. 39)

   A. What words would you use to describe the corporate personality of the board of which you are a member?

   B. What do the terms "autonomous" and "collaborative" imply in describing the behavior of your board membership?

2. Regardless of whether a board refers to itself as *trustees* or *directors* . . . the trust obligation is paramount. (p. 42)

   A. Who are the stakeholders in your organization? With what have they entrusted your board?

   B. How does your board deal with conflicts of interest and dual loyalties?

   C. Describe an example of board behavior as mismanagement (the failure to manage adequately), or nonmanagement (the failure to manage at all).

   D. How does your board demonstrate its trust obligations?

3. Board members who trust each other will also hold each other accountable for behaving corporately, rather than autonomously. (p. 45)

   A. How do you hold each other accountable as members of the board?

   B. Who has the responsibility of dealing with an inappropriately behaving board member?

4. The principle of *delegated authority/retained responsibility* deals with the roles and relationship of board and staff. (p. 47)

   A. What authority has been delegated by your board to your executive? What is your executive not authorized to do?

   B. Describe examples of board micromanaging and macromanaging?

5. The act of volunteering is an assertion of individual worth. (p. 50)

   A. What gifts and skills do you and other members bring to your board?

6 VOICE

To weaken the multiplicity of viewpoints would be to rob the board of its richness of wisdom. To weaken the unity of voice would be to rob the board of its opportunity for effectiveness.

John Carver

Several years ago, a brief news item in the *Tulsa World* newspaper told a fascinating story. It had to do with the city's Sales Tax Overview Committee (STOC), a group of volunteers organized to advise the city council. While not technically a Corporate Person, the committee members' accountability to each other had many similarities to board dynamics.

The news report was about an 80-year-old veteran member who had served 10 years on the STOC. While some colleagues called him "the committee's most knowledgeable person," the majority of the members had voted to recommend that the city council remove him. The problem was that he talked too much.

"Because of his destructive and disruptive behavior, Mr. C___ should be removed from STOC," said the petition, signed by 11 of the 15 members. He "continually makes personal attacks on former and current STOC members. He has stated verbally and in writing that the STOC should be eliminated. [He] continues to violate STOC bylaws by unauthorized communications with public officials, the media and the public."

"[He] communicates with the press, implying that he speaks for the whole committee," said one member. "No way would I speak for any one of you," said Mr. C___. "You're not worth speaking for."

After presenting the petition to the city council, the committee chair commented that it was a shame to seek dismissal of such a knowledgeable person. "This is his life. He spends 30 or 40 hours a week working on this. But he just can't keep his foot out of his mouth. It's really sad."[1]

It's really sad when the situation surfaces in volunteer boards, too. How does the Corporate Person speak? What should the "corporate mouth" be saying? Who is authorized to be the corporate voice and speak on behalf of the board?

Speaking to the public

The voice of an individual member disagreeing in public with decisions of the board gives an image of ineffective, dysfunctional corporate thinking. Additionally, it serves to break down the confidence of the organization's clients and stakeholders and to discredit its mission. It does little to encourage public support, financial or otherwise, for the organization.

As divided as board members may be in healthy and vigorous discussion over a particular issue, once the decision is made it becomes the board's decision. It's the will of the corporate mind, and having committed to that decision, the Corporate Person needs to interpret that decision with one voice to those who need to know. To do otherwise is to invite—at a minimum—personal and corporate embarrassment, the creation of rumors, and the criticism of constituents.[2]

Who speaks for the board? Legally, the minutes of board meetings are the only voice the Corporate Person has. The minutes interpret the collective thought and actions of the board, identifying those who participated and, perhaps more importantly, those who were absent during the meeting.

A more difficult question is "Who interprets what the minutes say?" It's risky to have each member of the board taking it upon herself or himself to speak for the board outside of meetings. Boards need to establish policy that authorizes one or more representatives who normally will interpret the actions and decisions of the board. This corporate voice policy is extremely important in order to provide mutual understanding, clarity of procedure, and consistency of interpretation for board members. Such a policy also serves to avoid breaches of confidentiality and potential legal entanglements.

A word about confidentiality is particularly important here. The Corporate Person needs to know when to keep its mouth shut! Confidentiality is essential to maintaining the full faith and confidence of the organization. Members should not discuss private deliberations of the board in public or subject other board members to embarrassment by criticizing them or their positions. Neither should they use their insider knowledge to betray confidences by speaking on behalf of the board without authorization, to gain some status, attention, or ego-gratification. That means not speaking to the media, staff, personal acquaintances, or the general public. Policy and procedures regarding confidentiality should both be in place and then regularly reviewed as a part of the ethical commitment of individual members to the corporate voice.

Privacy is the prerogative of the Corporate Person. Most not-for-profit volunteer boards are not bound by open meeting rules or the public's "right-to-know" unless specifically mandated by the bylaws of the organization. At the same time, closed meetings and executive sessions should be infrequent and need to be handled with particular discretion. Obviously, there are times when closed sessions are warranted, such as when dealing with personnel matters or pending litigation. However, when these situations are warranted, the Corporate Person needs to know how the flow of information is managed, who communicates actions, who speaks to those for whom the board's decisions may have personal implications, and who speaks to the media, who may also be eager to know.

In all circumstances, there needs to be a clear voice representing the collective mind of the Corporate Person; someone who speaks with the authority of the full board. Most often, this responsibility rests with the board chair or the executive leader. Nevertheless, whether it is board action and policy that needs interpretation by the chair, or whether it is an explanation of administrative implementation and technical information by the executive, neither speaks as the voice of the Corporate Person unless that is the will of the full board as established and authorized by board policy.

Others may also be spokespersons for the board. If the organization is large enough to employ a public relations staff person, that individual can be a valuable and skilled resource as the "corporate mouth." If a committee has had a major role in board policy or action, the chair of that committee or one of its members may be asked to be the board's voice. If a crisis has given rise to the need for public information, a member of the board who has been involved in crisis management or damage control may be the appropriate person to speak on the board's behalf. Finally, particularly when speaking to the media, the person who speaks for the board needs to be someone who knows how to provide clear, concise information in a form that will help a reporter understand and interpret accurately.

Board members who are singled out by the media or others, and pressured to give their own opinions or interpretations in a way that might be taken to represent the corporate voice, should refer their questioner to the board or staff member who is authorized and prepared to be a spokesperson. Again, policy is the key to controlling the corporate voice. Media policy ought to state clearly who talks to the press. This applies to staff as well as board members, and both groups must be aware of such a policy. When information is shared, "an organization . . . needs to speak with one voice, not 50 [voices]."[3]

There are times, of course, when individual members of a board are going to speak on behalf of their organization. Whenever possible, they ought to speak positively and enthusiastically about their organization's mission, vision, and programs. The public expects no less from those they recognize as members of a board. If there is credibility and trust in those individuals, respect for the organization is going to be enhanced and support generated.

Ideally, the voice of the Corporate Person speaking to the public should create a good image, representing the best the corporate body has to offer. That voice ought to reflect the spirit of volunteerism and commitment to the values that are the organization's corporate soul. Board members thinking and speaking corporately are at their best when working for the common good, sharing collective wisdom in order to make good decisions, presenting an effective public image, and telling their organization's story consistently, enthusiastically, and effectively. To insure consistency in what members of the board say to the public, one useful technique is to develop interpretive statements. These statements may be developed by staff or board personnel to help the entire board speak with one voice, rather than offering a number of personal interpretations.

However, there is a difference between speaking on behalf of the organization and speaking for the board. The rule still applies: "Without the board, you're *not* the board" . . . even if the public thinks you are. No individual board member should give anyone the impression that he or she can unilaterally speak for the board, make decisions, or change policy.

That difference is most frequently tested when a board member is confronted with complaints about the organization, its staff, or board actions. The complaints may come from individuals or groups of people who see the board member as someone who can remedy a situation. At times a well-meaning board member may assume that role, even inviting people to bring problems or complaints. However, giving the impression that an individual board member can do something about those problems or complaints breaks down the concept of the Corporate Person because that board member has no authority to speak for the collective body. Without the board, the individual member is only a concerned, involved volunteer with the interests of the organization at heart, but with no authority. Then what does the member who gets a complaint say if he or she can't speak with the corporate voice? The normal procedure follows these steps:

- Listen to the complainant but don't affirm the validity of the complaint, since all of the facts and both sides of the issue are probably not known.
- Don't give complainants the impression that now "they have the board on their side" or make promises that can't be kept by committing the board to some course of action.

- Refer the complainant to the executive director, who is normally in the best position to deal with the complaint, and who has the professional skills and authority to do so.
- Alert the executive to the potential problem or complaint, not with the weight of board authority, but as a concerned individual who happens to be a board member.
- Do not bring the complaint to a board meeting unless it is of significant severity to warrant board action. The basic rule is "no surprises" at board meetings—either for the executive or other members of the board.
- Expect executive leadership to deal with the problem or complaint or, if warranted, to bring the situation to the board with alternative problem-solving proposals.

Board members who refrain from speaking unilaterally—and who understand the importance of speaking corporately—can relieve themselves of a great deal of stress and effort; a burden they do not have to bear individually when they realize they speak more effectively as the Corporate Person. Andrew Swanson's recommendation is right on target: "If you are ever in doubt as to the propriety of your speaking in circumstances wherein your words may be interpreted as the word of the board, the best advice is—don't!"[4]

SPEAKING TO EACH OTHER

The corporate voice is not only used for communicating with the public. That voice is also heard in the deliberations, flow of information, and exchange of ideas around the board table. The analogy of an old-time switchboard operator has been used to describe the Corporate Person as a manager of communications. Words are the board's particular commodity and information is shared by the board both externally, from and to the public, and internally, from and to the organization. To do all of that, the members need to be at the switchboard—the board table—talking to each other.

What do the voices that make up the corporate voice sound like? Around the table, there is variety: the knowledgeable voices, the respectful, the well-prepared, the assertive, and the opinionated. There are thoughtful ones, the quiet, the shy, and the "dysfunctionally polite" ones. There may also be ambivalent, uninformed, or apathetic voices, although they usually don't say much. There are probably voices from a diverse mix of perspectives and experience, education, social, and economic backgrounds. If the board is truly inclusive, there will be a balance of masculine and feminine voices, and those representative of various racial, cultural, and ethnic backgrounds.

One fairly universal characteristic of the voices of the board is that there will be some who are dominant and others who are more submissive. Some are more adversarial, others are more conciliatory. The challenge in any board is to respect and blend those voices rather than creating a cacophony!

In the center of all that talk, with a hand on the switchboard, is one member—the board chair—whose role is crucial to the process. The chair speaks not only for but to the board. Formidable tasks require that the board chair be a leader capable of thinking and speaking from the perspective of the corporate voice. Those tasks include developing an agenda, presiding over meetings, coordinating committee functions, encouraging active participation of members, managing conflict productively, communicating effectively with executive staff, and maintaining both discipline and high morale among board members.

Disagreement, debate, and divergence over issues happens regularly around the board table, and well it should. If consideration of various options and alternatives is going to take place in the process of planning, policy development, and informed decision making, the variety of voices needs to be heard. While someone has observed that "If two board members agree about everything, one of them probably isn't necessary!" it may be that some members need permission to disagree. "Dysfunctional politeness" is a cultural trait that prevents some individuals from pursuing information necessary to make good decisions because they are reluctant to ask hard questions or challenge opinions.

The role of the board is to be hard question-askers. Members need to know that they have permission to do that in ways that will be productive in the process of corporate thinking and deciding. A culture where debate is expected and divergent viewpoints are respected creates a climate for the corporate voice to speak clearly when decisions are made.

That assumes the individual voices are tempered by some civility, of course. Char Mollison, vice president of Independent Sector, has pointed out that "despite the dangers of over-politeness, boards must often deal with the opposite problem—the rude board member whose behavior has troublesome consequences for the organization."[5] That kind of voice, exemplified by Mr. C___ of Tulsa at the beginning of this chapter, leads to dissonance and disharmony, not clarity and confidence, when the Corporate Person speaks. When and if that happens, it becomes the board's responsibility to bring a recalcitrant member under control. That can be done through rules of order at the meeting, a private conversation with the board chair, peer pressure from other members, or, in extreme circumstances, whatever formal action is permitted by the organization's bylaws for removing the disruptive and discordant voice.

A number of suggestions are helpful for board members in speaking to each other around the board table:

- Come prepared to participate. Board members don't speak articulately by pooling ignorance.
- Practice the "no surprises" rule. Issues to be discussed should be introduced by inclusion on an agenda, not dropped in as unlisted and undocumented items of new business.
- Make an effort to share thoughts or ask questions about at least one agenda item at each meeting.
- Keep an open mind in the debate over issues. Committing to a particular outcome before engaging in discussion damages the board decision-making process.
- Use "I" language rather than "you" language in debating controversial issues. An adversarial or accusatory voice creates more smoke and heat than light!
- Focus on *what* the problem is, rather than *who* the problem is. Personality conflicts always color and cloud the issue and make objectivity difficult.
- Allow no disagreement on issues to result in personal animosity outside board meetings.
- Publicly support board decisions through the corporate voice once the debate is concluded and action taken.

SPEAKING TO EXECUTIVE AND STAFF

In *Boards That Make A Difference*, John Carver describes the voices of the board as "a forum of churning debate and exposure, an exciting place," adding, "This debate and exposure of course must concern the big questions rather than the small ones, the results rather than the methods. This is definitely not staff work, though staff members will undoubtedly have ideas to contribute. In fact, involving both board and staff here causes no problem. As long as roles are clearly defined, the board can invite staff to join in the fun. The board is not being pulled downward to staff-level concerns; rather, the staff is stretched upward to board-level concerns, though as guests in the process, not its masters. As thinking, caring human beings, staff members have much to contribute to the dialogue, and everyone profits by their being invited to do so."[6]

Much has been written about the continuing need to define the proper roles of board and staff. Board members need to understand the distinct role they fill. (See the section on *delegated authority/retained responsibility* in chapter 4.) The best relationship is that of a collaborative team, with staff and the board communicating articulately and appropriately.

The corporate voice of the board needs to speak clearly to the executive leader and through the executive to the rest of the staff. Collectively, the board speaks in a formal way to the executive through its basic established, written policies. For example, executive-limitation policies are those that set boundaries beyond which the executive cannot act without board approval (for example, "The executive will not make expenditures of more than $5,000 without board authorization"). In speaking this way, the board says to the executive, "We trust you to act responsibly within those limits; stay within the budget and policy we've established, get the work done, and we'll monitor the progress based on accomplishment rather than micromanaging."

The board must also agree with the executive on what needs to be accomplished. Policy in this case takes the form of goals that are developed through a collaborative planning process. Until there is clear agreement on where the board wants the organization to go, and the corporate voice articulates that direction, it will be very difficult for the executive to propose ways of getting there. Boards and their executive leaders are motivated by accomplishment, not muddling. That requires good communication. Therefore beyond formal policy language, good, informal conversation between individual members and their executive leader is essential both for building trust and for gathering information. Furthermore, private one-on-one conversation is certainly appropriate: between the executive and the board chair, the secretary or treasurer of the board, members of committees and task forces, and others in the context of getting work done.

Nevertheless two cautions may be in order, lest the corporate voice be muted. Informal conversations such as those just referred to should never carry overtones of board supervision. The executive must be accountable to and supervised by the full board, not any individual. "No board member has authority over the CEO. *No* member. That includes the board chair. A CEO who is supervised by or reports to the chair is not a true CEO. For the CEO by definition works for the whole board. . . . Well-intentioned board chairs can themselves destroy the board's obligation to speak with one voice to its CEO, often due to a . . . motivation either to exercise quasi-CEO authority or to be more responsible than the board."[7]

On the other hand, individual board members speaking with their executive need to understand that there is a fine line between personal friendship and support, and the member's role as part of the Corporate Person. The obligation of the board is to the best interests of the organization. That supersedes loyalties a member may have to the executive when the corporate voice sets limits or gives direction. Thus, for one or more members of the board to take it upon themselves to be a "support group" for the executive may give the impression of favoritism, confuse board and staff roles, and affect the ability of the corporate voice to speak directly. It also invites the executive to do board business with a few favored members, rather than speaking to the board as a whole.

When the executive speaks to the board and the board speaks to the executive, what does the corporate conversation sound like? A fundamental principle in such interaction is that the board doesn't exist to advise staff on how to do their work; staff exist to assist the board in making decisions and giving direction to the organization. Through the executive, staff provide options, advice, and alternative solutions to the board. That's what staff, in their professional capacity, are hired to do. Individual board members who have the capacity, skill, and expertise to advise the staff on how to do their work become quasi-staff themselves at that point and step out of their governing role.

Again, board members are to be question-askers, not answer-givers. They should not try to provide answers to operational difficulties and should never accept from staff the upward delegation of problems. "Don't bring us problems, bring us alternative solutions," is what the corporate voice needs to say to the executive.[8] An insightful board member articulated this principle clearly when he told his executive, "Don't ask me what I think. Ask me what I think about what you think and then we'll get something done!"[9]

I watched an executive do an upward delegation of problems to a committee of his board. "We've got this awkward situation in our eastern area office," he said, and went on to describe the "awkward situation" in great and gory detail. Having done that, he excused himself, apologized for having to go to another meeting, and left with the request that the committee decide what to do about the problem. Baffled, the committee members spent the next hour pooling their ignorance, and returned to the board meeting with no solutions at all.

The least the executive might have done was suggest a possible course of action. If he couldn't stay to offer his professional advice and perspectives, at least he should have spelled out the alternatives that the committee needed to consider. Of course, the problem should have been handed back to the executive to deal with if the situation didn't require board action.

The basic question for the corporate voice to ask is "What are our options?" The response from executive leadership should be in the form of recommendations including, if possible, alternative solutions. To offer only one solution leaves the board with the decision simply to say "yes" or "no" rather than to weigh alternatives and implications. To offer a range of options (including a clear indication of which option the executive prefers) gives the corporate voice of the board something to discuss and debate. In the course of that discussion, the board also needs to be sure that staff has a plan for implementing the recommendation. Implementation is not the board's responsibility, but being assured that their decision can be implemented certainly is.

In considering alternative solutions, several additional questions get to the heart of the matter:[10]

- *Can we change direction if this option proves to be a mistake?* Note that reversible decisions can be made fairly quickly but irreversible decisions take more thought and time.
- *What may we lose if we choose this option?* Worst-case scenarios are important. And even if there is a short-term loss, is there a long-term gain?
- *Can we interpret our decision adequately to our stakeholders?* Here is where case statements are important for the corporate voice.
- *What potential problems does the choice of this option pose?* Problems are more easily dealt with when they are anticipated.
- *How much control will we have as our choice of options is implemented?* The ability to monitor progress and make midcourse corrections is an essential part of the planning process.

Collaborative board and staff communication always means dialogue, with a free flow of information. A few observations on that subject close this chapter on the corporate voice.

The habit of some boards is to routinely go into an executive session that excludes their executive. While that practice may heighten the sense of solidarity and authority of the Corporate Person, it creates a kind of *Wizard of Oz* atmosphere as the executive waits nervously outside for words of wisdom or judgment to be handed down from "on high." It's a bad idea because it breaks down confidence and communication with the executive. The secrecy involved generates speculation and rumors, and the reality of a collaborative board-staff team is broken by the impression of top-down arrogance.

With regard to communication board members may have with other staff, it is important for the board to let staff know that the executive has the confidence and backing of the board. Consequently, while the board shouldn't hesitate to compliment and encourage staff, board members should never get into triangulated situations between staff and the executive, inviting either critique or comment on the executive's work or on staff relations with the executive. It should be assumed that staff, through their organizational structure, have access to the executive and that on occasion certain staff will be involved with the board—at the invitation and direction of the executive—for specific assistance and advice to the board. It also needs to be understood that staff relate to the board only through the executive or with the executive's knowledge.

Critical comment or complaints from staff should be handled by the board in the same way as board members handle external complaints from the public—with the added guidance of internal personnel policies, which contain grievance procedures for staff to follow. The one glaring gap in many grievance procedures is in the case of midlevel management having a complaint about the executive, where appealing to the next level of supervision means bringing the complaint to the person who allegedly is the source of the grievance. Boards, in their establishment of policy, need to provide for that contingency—although to be a court of appeal for staff should be only a last resort for extreme cases and never done without the knowledge of the executive.

A word is also in order about staff involvement in executive evaluation. The board's corporate responsibility is to review executive performance. Some boards are inclined to invite staff to be involved in that process to provide critical or constructive comment. To do that is usually inappropriate if lines of authority within the staffing structure of the organization are to be maintained. It puts the board in the unacceptable position of soliciting direct comments from staff about their executive. It also puts staff in the awkward position of critiquing a supervisor who must make executive decisions relative to their performance and employment. Since the board establishes the criteria for the measurement of executive performance, they have the responsibility for doing the measuring. They should not delegate that to staff or anyone else.

In these instances, as in all of the board's work, the strong voice of the Corporate Person is critical to communicating its mind and soul, and to affirming its corporate behavior.

1. How does the Corporate Person speak? What should the "corporate mouth" be saying? (p. 53)

   A. Who is authorized to speak as the corporate voice for the board of which you are a member?

   B. What are your board's policies and procedures in responding to complaints made to individual members? Are those policies implemented appropriately?

2. What do the voices that make up the corporate voice sound like? Around the table, there is variety . . . (p. 57)

   A. How does a board tone down its dominant voices and draw out its submissive voices so that the voice of the corporate person comes to represent the opinions of all the members?

   B. What problems occur in your board meetings when members are dysfunctionally polite?

3. The corporate voice of the board needs to speak clearly to the executive leader and through the executive to the rest of the staff. (p. 60)

   A. How does your board demonstrate its corporate role in giving direction to the executive?

   B. Give an example of the upward delegation of problems in communication between staff and board. How does your board assure that alternate solutions are presented?

   C. What is the authorized role of the executive committee of your board? When, if ever, does it speak or decide for the full board?

   D. How does your board make use of evaluation/performance review to speak with and to your executive? How does the board ensure that the process is constructive and mutually beneficial?

7 HEALTH

Autoiesis . . . its meaning has been imprinted on my consciousness: "The characteristic of living systems to continuously renew themselves and to regulate this process in such a way that the integrity of their structure is maintained." Autopoiesis—natural processes that support the quest for structure, process, renewal, integrity. This description is not limited to one type of organism—it describes life itself.

Margaret Wheatley

Like any complex organism, the creature called the Corporate Person can survive, even for an extended period, without good health. But quality of life means more than mere survival. It means growth and change and renewed vitality.

In *Leadership and the New Science*, Margaret Wheatley establishes as a fundamental premise the idea that "every living thing expends energy and will do whatever is needed to preserve itself, including changing."[1] That applies to organizations and extends to the concept of the Corporate Person.

Although an "artificial person," a creature of law, the Corporate Person has a life of its own. That group of "natural persons" entrusted with the governance of an organization is collectively engaged in maintaining the state of the Corporate Person's health—its wellness, energy, relative strength or weakness—*and* its ability to change and adapt. The Corporate Person must continually attend to those needs. Health maintenance and management is an ongoing concern.

Change can be painful. Consequently, the corporate body is rarely pain-free. That's a fact of life. The question is: "How does the Corporate Person cope with pain—including the acute, immediate hurt of crises; uncertainty about the future; external threats; and internal disruptions?" It also embraces the chronic suffering caused by long-term ingrained bad board habits, cultural dysfunction, and weak leadership. Is the pain dealt with by getting angry or by trying to ignore it? By feeling stress, anxiety, discouragement, or depression? All of those reactions manifest themselves in corporate thinking and behavior. Just as in individual attitudes, they weaken the corporate body.

Health for the Corporate Person means expending effort to work for wholeness and build new vitality. A healthy board doesn't ignore pain or act as though it doesn't exist. Neither does it simply go on talking about its poor health without doing something. It recognizes the symptoms, then goes to work to find positive solutions and treatment.

As with individual persons, the Corporate Person experiences a difference between "pain" and "suffering." A suffering Corporate Person does little or nothing to react to pain. It simply accepts the idea that board work "is a pain." Threats and dysfunctional behavior become part of a sick corporate culture. Prolonged unwillingness to deal with conflict; ignored warnings and challenges from the external environment; refusal to learn, change, or grow with the times; failure to monitor or even to take responsibility . . . all of that becomes self-inflicted, internalized, chronic suffering, and that's not healthy![2]

A Corporate Person's pain, on the other hand, may be exactly what alerts its body, mind, and soul to the need to react. Pain can't be avoided, but if it alerts the board to trouble it can produce a healthy response. "One indication of a healthy group is its ability to transform conflict into creative problem-solving. All groups must protect themselves . . . from disruptive forces from the outside and disorganizing forces from within. . . . Cohesive groups are more likely to defend themselves against threats. Further, they permit greater expression of hostility. In cohesive groups, there is a powerful sense of loyalty and the members are important enough to each other that they are willing to bear the discomfort of working through conflict."[3]

Board self-assessment: Looking for health

One study points out that "the mature group is willing to examine itself in a nondefensive manner if it is to grow and develop. The healthy group must assume responsibility for diagnosing its own problems and changing its procedures or processes, if necessary. Healthy groups are those in which group members feel accepted, safe to express their opinions without fear of reprisal, and in which conflict is acknowledged and dealt with in an open and constructive manner. It pays close attention to its vital maintenance function and will develop through various stages of its life cycle. Its health is related to its ability to integrate and work toward group goals."[4]

Regular corporate self-assessment is a task too often postponed or avoided. Many boards resist any regular, routine checkup or scheduled examination of their health. What they don't realize is that if they neglect to intentionally and regularly evaluate themselves as a corporate body, evaluation will still occur. It will happen informally and erratically in the hallways and on the sidewalks after the board meetings. It will happen as individual members talk to each other about executive performance and board-staff interaction. It will happen as the board does its planning and critiques its progress or lack of progress. It will happen as community, staff, and client complaints filter back to the board.

These informal evaluations are counterproductive because they are often unmanageable and may deteriorate into festering gripe sessions, frustration, and demoralization. While some boards may avoid self-assessment because it might involve self-criticism or critiquing of peers, that kind of pain is minimal compared to the illness and injury that may result without regular, intentional examination and evaluation.

Consider some of the excuses and counterarguments for regular evaluation:

Excuse: Evaluation and self-assessment imply criticism, focusing on deficiencies and shortcomings.

Response: Done right, they ought to focus on affirming strength as well as correcting weaknesses.

Excuse: Boards have such limited time. Self-assessment cuts into valuable meeting time where the *real* work goes on.

Response: It doesn't have to take hours of time once the board gets a system and process in place for annual review.

Excuse: It's unfair to subject the efforts of volunteers to critical review.
Response: Board responsibilities are too important not to critique!

Excuse: We're not sure what to evaluate, how to do it, or who should facilitate the process.

Response: That can be learned; resources abound.

Excuse: Self-assessment can be threatening to our ego (collectively and individually).

Response: Ego shouldn't be involved; good evaluation deals with "what" and "how," not "who."

Excuse: This board is made up of leaders who certainly are capable and know what they are doing.

Response: Real leaders know the importance of collaborative corporate assessment.

Excuse: We've just never given much thought to doing an evaluation of ourselves.

Response: Maybe it's high time you did!

And the number 1 excuse: We're doing just fine. This is a great board!
Response: Who says so? What are your criteria for measuring greatness?

That number 1 excuse lifts up a basic principle for evaluation and review, not only as a board does self-assessment but as it does any kind of monitoring: Measurement can be done only against established criteria and standards. The guiding principle for evaluation is: "Don't ask how things are unless you have first said how things ought to be."[5] The first self-assessment activity of any board should be agreement about what a "great" board looks like; what a healthy Corporate Person's vital signs are in terms of growth, strength, and effectiveness. Then the assessment can begin.[6]

The assessment may be self-guided, either by the whole board or an authorized committee. It may have a more structured retreat format, using an outside facilitator with special skills, objectivity, and time-management ability to guide the process. Another approach is to do a peer-assessment, using a former board member or a respected peer from another organization to observe and provide evaluative commentary and feedback.

Board assessment may be as simple as a brief, informal discussion at the end of a board meeting (a 10-minute analysis) with several open-ended questions, such as "What are we doing well?" "What are we missing?" and "What should be our standards for improvement?" At the other end of the scale, assessments can also use complex meta-analysis formats led by consultants, using complex measurement instruments and diagnostic tools. Every board needs to determine how much time is appropriate to invest in assessment. There is no single right way to do it and the only mistake is to *not* do it!

There are five basic approaches to board assessments.[7] The most common is the *organizational assessment*, which evaluates and measures the board in terms of its mission, values, plans, programs, policies, and goals. This normally happens in conjunction with measuring program accomplishment and monitoring the organization's planning process. This type of assessment deals with basic questions of purpose: Why do we exist? Where are we going? Are we getting there? The healthy board periodically reviews those fundamental questions.

A second type is the *cultural/behavioral assessment.* In this self-examination, the board looks at its corporate personality, work style, identity, and internal effectiveness. It seeks to measure how it "does the right things" against established standards of basic board behavior (see chapter 5).

The third type of assessment deals with *roles, responsibilities, and functions.* It analyzes the board's health by reviewing the mandates and authority for its existence—its articles of incorporation and bylaws, policies, job descriptions, organizational structure, relationships with stakeholders, and governance principles. This assessment measures the board's health in terms of doing its work "the right way."

Meeting assessment is a fourth approach. Usually, it is done at the end of board meetings. It specifically deals with measuring the effectiveness of meetings, analyzing the way the board corporately does its work in specific sessions of authorized and recorded board activity.

A fifth approach, the *personal board member assessment,* although dealing with subjective attitudes, provides an attitudinal check on how individual members feel about their contributions, participation, and interaction with other board members, and their personal commitment to the health of the corporate body.

The most compelling reason for board self-assessment is to maintain corporate health by demonstrating willing accountability and good stewardship. These are issues of wellness not only for the body, but also the mind and soul of the Corporate Person. Self-assessment can be a positive, constructive, educational experience. Through it the board becomes more aware of its role in leading and governing an organization, as well as dealing with obstacles and barriers to effective performance. It requires commitment to the process by all the members, particularly the executive staff leader, board chair, and the committee authorized to set up the process, coordinate the activity, analyze the results, and provide follow-up action.

Self-assessment has the potential for shaping the board's corporate personality and culture, building a base of expectations and performance standards for its future, and providing an environment for board education and development. All of these are important factors in maintaining the Corporate Person's health and well-being.

VITAL SIGNS

Board self-assessment is a continuing diagnostic process, necessary because board members come and go and because situations, times, and needs change.

What should come from this diagnosis? What may be discovered in the process? My personal analogy is that of going to the doctor for an annual checkup, an event for which I can think of any number of procrastinating excuses for postponing. But the doctor's scale, blood pressure cuff, and blood tests are important. I want to know the results from the readings because I want to know what good health looks like. Not that the numbers in themselves mean anything—the number of pounds on the scale, pulse rate, systolic and diastolic blood pressure measurements, or the readings from my lipid panel. But when I'm told what the normal range is between overweight and underweight, between hyper- and hypo-tension, and what the acceptable numbers for cholesterol and triglyceride levels are, then I have something to measure against. I begin to understand something about my vital signs—the indicators not only of what shape I'm in, but what condition I ought to be in to be really healthy. That gives me something to work at, and corrective measures to take with professional help if need be.

If the Corporate Person is really healthy, what should the vital signs look like? Here is a sampling using the categories described in chapters 2–6 of this book.

Corporate body: a strong Person, with a vigorous, collaborative group of members working together as one person for the common good. Vital signs include:

- members recruited and elected with attention to particular skills and gifts.
- a high degree of personal commitment by the members to their roles and functions, and to the mission of the organization.
- mutual respect of the members for each other and for executive leadership.
- an awareness that together the members are the board, but that individually they are not the board.
- a clear sense of fiduciary responsibility—with a commitment to legal, financial, and ethical integrity.

Corporate soul: an honorable Person, whose members have a common vision, values, mission, and a well-developed corporate conscience. Vital signs include:

- a mission statement that is visible, inspirational, and operative in decision making and in implementation of programs and services.
- defined values that articulate the board's core beliefs, guiding principles, and philosophy of governance.
- visionary leadership shared by the board and executive leader.
- legal and ethical trustworthiness that is seen as an obligation to stakeholders and the public.
- a corporate conscience evidenced by the ongoing accountability of the board to its constituency.

Corporate mind: an intelligent Person, whose members are capable of thinking collectively, developing plans, and making good decisions that are remembered, established, and practiced through policy. Vital signs include:

- meetings of the board that have adequate preparation and full participation of members.
- commitment to discussion, debate, and decision making as a collaborative group process.

- decisions, once made, that are respected as representing the will of the Corporate Person.
- functional and effective monitoring, evaluating, and projecting of plans as a primary board activity.
- board policies compiled and available for ready reference.
- continuing education, information sharing, and member skill-development that is a routine part of board activity.
- institutional memory preserved through written history and well-kept archives of documents and other materials.

Corporate behavior: a responsible Person, whose diverse members act collectively for a common purpose in a trustworthy and accountable manner, understanding that the authority they delegate to others is a responsibility that they ultimately must retain for themselves. Vital signs include:
- a corporate culture of mutual trust and accountability.
- board members from diverse backgrounds working effectively together for the good of the organization.
- an attitude of respect for the combined strength and ability of the board that comes through collaborative action rather than autonomous disregard for group process.
- effective orientation of members to their roles and responsibilities.
- avoidance of micromanaging through an understanding of the board's governance role, in partnership with and relation to the operational role of executive and staff.
- clear delegation of authority in the form of job descriptions, board policy, and formal actions of the board.
- conscientious effort to avoid mismanagement and nonmanagement by active participation and adherence to policy and legal requirements.
- awareness of the stakeholders to whom the board is ultimately accountable through their obligation of trust.

Corporate voice: an articulate Person, whose members communicate appropriately, representing the views, decisions, and image of the organization in a positive manner. Vital signs include:
- maintenance of a good public image by members individually and corporately affirming the organization.
- public support generated through the credibility and trust of board members.
- clear information management and communication, both internally and externally.

- lively questioning and debate over options and alternative courses of action proposed for board decision making.
- respect for confidentiality among board members.
- interpretation of corporate decisions and actions through a designated spokesperson.
- strong working relationships between the board and the executive leader that are established by job descriptions, annual goals, evaluation, and regular interaction in an atmosphere of trust and mutual respect.
- appropriate interaction of board and staff.
- policy for handling complaints understood and implemented effectively.

This list of vital signs for the health of the Corporate Person is by no means exhaustive. However, any board can take these generalizations as a starting point. In detail that fits their organization, board members can make them specific by discussing and describing expectations they have for their own life together. That exercise is a significant way of caring, nurturing, and maintaining vitality.

Health maintenance: Keeping pace with change

In a rapidly changing environment, the Corporate Person may be subjected to one identity crisis after another. "Who am I? Why am I here?" Those memorable rhetorical questions asked by Reform Party vice-presidential candidate James Stockdale during the 1992 political campaign debates are echoed in not-for-profit board rooms across the country.

"Who are we? Why are we here?" Asked corporately, they are important questions for warding off institutional amnesia. The reasons an organization came into existence, the vision of the founders and the historical events that have sustained and empowered the life of the organization must not be forgotten. To forget is to risk an unhealthy loss of commitment on the part of present board members.

An equally important question is "Where are we going?" Faced with funding cutbacks, new political realities, challenges to tax exempt status, the need for partnerships and collaborations, corporate restructuring, pressure for mergers, and changing societal values and needs, the Corporate Person has ample reason to feel some anxiety about its future. History and institutional memory may provide a solid foundation to stand on, but what brings stability and strength when the winds of change blow so hard that they threaten the life, health, and well-being of the Corporate Person? The operative answer is *organizational continuity*—a matter requiring the board's constant attention. It takes a variety of forms.

For many organizations, *continuity of constituent relationships* is primary. Without the continued support of those who have a stake in the organization's mission, who have shaped the organization's values, and who look to the organization for support and programs and services, there is little reason to go on living. Without a constituent group—to whom the board is accountable and which holds the board in trust and may elect the members of the corporate body—the Corporate Person will die a slow death, continuing for a while only by the sheer momentum of past accomplishments. Constituent relationships can never be taken for granted, regardless of changes in funding sources or the attraction of potential partners who may have different constituencies, mission, or values. The board must pay attention to its trust obligations for the sake of the Corporate Person's very existence. To do otherwise is to commit corporate suicide, to give up or give away what the Corporate Person is obligated to nurture and protect.

Internally, the board must also be concerned with *continuity of policy and programs.* That requires an ongoing, proactive planning process that anticipates change and shapes governing policies that give consistent direction. Although individual board members may come and go, those policies provide a common understanding of the organization's board process, give guidance to the executive leadership, and minimize redeliberation of decisions already made. Due diligence and fiduciary responsibility require that all members of the Corporate Person live within that structure of consistent policy. Although programmatically the organization may change radically as times demand, the underlying consistency of commitment to the organization's mission, vision, and values remains, providing a continuity that permits the Corporate Person to grow and move with the times.

Continuity of quality is another concern. Chapter 2 described the elements that provide corporate quality of life. Assuring the continuation of personal, legal, ethical, and spiritual quality in the Corporate Person is essential. Without those life-giving elements, the organization loses its focus, integrity, and character, and its programs and services will diminish in the process. Strength and health is preserved and enhanced when the board monitors and evaluates its own quality through self-assessment. Continuity of quality is also assured as the board insists on the organization's compliance with requirements of regulatory bodies and the highest professional, educational, and programmatic standards of accrediting bodies. Continuity also comes through employing qualified and trained staff who manage a quality review process that monitors and evaluates all aspects of the organization's operations and services. That review process, if it effectively informs the board, provides essential information for planning and policy making that contributes to the Corporate Person's vitality and strength.

Organizational continuity also means *continuity of board and executive leadership*. If it is concerned about its organization's future, the board must be involved in the succession of its members. Weak members mean diminished strength (see chapter 2). While an argument may be made for the stability of self-perpetuating boards with no rotation of members or term limits, there ought to be a genuine concern for the inherent dangers "in-breeding" brings to the health of the Corporate Person. Myopic and entrenched values, behaviors, and perspectives can be detrimental.

No one knows better than current board members what qualifications and characteristics are needed for future board leadership. For that reason, careful attention needs to be given to the nominating process; identification of characteristics and criteria; recruitment of potential members with needed skills, motivation, and commitment; and policies for term limitation and membership rotation.

Finally and of paramount importance, continuity of leadership means the *selection, supervision, strengthening, evaluation, and eventual replacement of the board's executive leader*. Without strength and proactive involvement in this relationship, the Corporate Person's effectiveness is in jeopardy. While many executives outlast an entire rotation of board members, chances are the executive's tenure will be shorter than the life-span of the Corporate Person, which has a continuing existence even though its members may come and go. Realistically, every board lives with the knowledge that there will be changes in executive leadership, whether through resignation, retirement, death, or termination. In anticipation of that change, policies that govern replacement that are well-thought-out in advance should be in place even while the current executive leader is in office. These may include board action for executive succession, interim management, internal staff promotion, executive job description, and executive performance review.[8]

Life cycles, growth, and maturity

Through all these changes and challenges, will the Corporate Person ever grow up? Is it possible for the governing board of a not-for-profit organization to reach a point of real maturity? The answer is "Perhaps."

Over time, the Corporate Person's corporate culture and personality will most certainly change. Given a degree of good health over years of growth, learning and coping with change, maturation of one sort or another will probably happen. *Autopoiesis* (Margaret Wheatley's word, defined at the beginning of this chapter) is a reality in every living system, including the Corporate Person.

Ichak Adizes, writing in *Organizational Passages*, describes the maturation process this way: "People, products, markets, even societies, have life cycles—birth, growth, maturity, old age, and death. At every life-cycle passage, a typical pattern of behavior emerges. As the organization passes from one phase of its life to the next, different roles are emphasized and the different role combinations that result produce a different organizational set of behaviors."[9]

As the Corporate Person changes, its personality, behavior, and self-image are going to change. That's normal and predictable. What aren't always predictable are the forces and influences that will produce change. Although the effects that external challenges and internal crises have on the Corporate Person's health may be pathological, they need not be. It depends on the strength, resilience, and intestinal fortitude of the Corporate Person. Whether corporate health is affected, one thing is certain: Its personality, culture, body, soul, mind, behavior, and voice are going to change. Human life cycles and corporate life cycles are alike in that way.

For the Corporate Person, the change from one stage of life to another happens with the growing awareness that a current mode of governing and behavior no longer works because it can't meet the demands and stresses placed upon it. Life cycle transitions require adjustments and adaptation in both leadership and organizational structure because what used to work well doesn't work anymore. Just as childlike (or childish) behavior is perfectly acceptable for the young, it's not at all appropriate as a person grows older and takes on responsibility in a more complicated world. So too, change is required when the Corporate Person faces challenges to its capabilities, behavior, and culture. That may be painful and even pathological, but how successfully the transitions are made will have great bearing on its health and vitality.

FIVE STAGES OF LIFE

Consider the Corporate Person's life cycle in terms of these five stages: childhood, adolescence, young adult, middle age, and honorary elder.

The childhood stage may take some organizations years to outgrow. It is the board in its earliest stage, in which a group of people led by a strong parental father or mother figure have gathered together and a new organization has been born. Its articles of incorporation proclaim that a new Corporate Person has come into being and they love this child they have formed. There's a strong commitment to it and the cause it will serve, even though there may be struggles in the early months or years to help it survive. There's no question that the founding parent, who may serve both as board chair and executive leader, is in charge. He or she is the moving force responsible for the organizing, planning, bill paying, money raising, and worrying. Other board members often voluntarily do much of the hands-on work for the agency since there aren't dollars available to hire help or hand out allowances, but it's fun.

At this stage, there's youthful exuberance, a lot of creativity, dreaming, and childlike idealism. Governing the organization is simple and informal. It is like a family with a young child that experiences tangible rewards, even if there is a skinned knee or elbow now and then. There are no organizational charts or committee structures. The board has little to do but be a helping part of the family because the founder-parent is making most of the decisions and giving the orders. Under that parent's watchful eye, this Corporate Person-child is nurtured and grows.

Then come challenges, crises, and change. More staff are hired; more programs and services are generated. New employees may not share the enthusiasm or perspectives of the founding board. The founding board may have difficulty backing away from the operational work it's been doing. The founder/parent/executive/board chair may get tired or become entrenched. Growth demands more structure, monitoring, planning, and responsibility. The times demand change.

The adolescent stage starts when the Corporate Person begins to think about what it might be "when it grows up." It looks at the organization it governs and, as board consultant Karl Mathiasen puts it, "picks up its socks and starts to take some responsibility."[10] The relationship between the board and the executive leader begins to be defined, although not without some testing and turmoil at times. It is not unlike a parent and teenager needing to define the lines of authority. At this point in the Corporate Person's life cycle, either policy has not been written, or it has not been clearly articulated to give direction and communication between board, staff, and others. Now the board is beginning to flex its muscles and understand its power to make decisions, even if it doesn't have a wealth of experience and may demonstrate some immaturity at times.

At this point, there may also be some reluctance on the part of the executive leader to let the board take responsibility—particularly if the executive is the "founding-parent" type. This is the stage where the board may begin to resist a top-down administrative style where the executive does most of its thinking. At the same time the executive, like the parent of a teenager, may not be sure when this Corporate Person-adolescent is ready to "take the wheel and learn to drive." The adolescent isn't sure, either. As Karl Mathiasen says, "Giving up and sharing power is one of the hardest tasks humans face, and, moreover, boards often find great comfort in following a leader and do not want to have the authority or responsibilities called for in the sharing of leadership."[11]

As its organizational programs and services grow, the adolescent Corporate Person begins to discover that it takes money to do the work. Budgets and fund-raising are important, as is good management. This means the board begins to give direction to the executive that may—in turn—result in meddling, interference, or micromanaging. It may at least be interpreted that way by the executive who may view it as an adolescent telling a parent what to do. There is some awkwardness and role confusion at this stage. However, learning is also happening, even if by trial and error.

The board is becoming a partner in the process of governance. Faced with new responsibilities, the Corporate Person-adolescent discovers new challenges, crises, and change. Corporate life isn't as simple as it was in childhood. Founding-parent leaders still have a strong claim on the organization and aren't sure they want to see their baby grow up. New challenges to the organization may require new leadership. Staff and board leaders begin to be replaced—not always without turmoil—and the board starts to take on a corporate identity of its own. The times are changing and so is the Corporate Person.

The young adult stage finds the Corporate Person stepping out into a complex world with an emerging awareness of its own identity. Its responsibilities include financial integrity; planning for the future; articulating a vision, values, and goals; making good decisions; assuming legal and ethical accountability; and staying healthy in the process. Meeting these are all indications of growing maturity.

This is a stage in the Corporate Person's life cycle where courtship in the form of partnerships and collaboration become important. Executive leadership may again have changed. Now the relationship with the board becomes a team approach. There is an emerging respect—even an admiration—for the skills and efforts of each of the partners. Although not fully mature or consistent, there is better communication among board members, executive leadership, and constituents. This Corporate Person-young adult implements management practices and formal policies and there is a businesslike approach to board work. The board's work is done "by the book" with committees in place and delegated authority.

There is also a growing awareness of other organizations, other Corporate Persons around them. Are they competitors or potential partners? Turf protection may become a value, as the board's strong sense of its mission, identity, and vision grows. At the same time, there may be an interest in those others. Is it possible they have something in common; even that some day they might find a strong mutual attraction leading to a merged identity?

The Corporate Person-young adult feels strong, vital, and important. It is ready to meet challenges, crises, and change; and they come with a vengeance. The pressure of competition; shifting political realities; increasing challenges to provide resources, vision, and plans that may exceed board and staff competence; and the discovery that the textbook approach to governance may need to be tempered by practical realities all abound. Change is everywhere present and the Corporate Person has to adapt and grow.

The middle-age stage is a point of maturity in the Corporate Person's life cycle. This assumes that it has survived the impact of change to this point, has learned from past experience, and has preserved a stability in its life through institutional memory and established policy.

It should be noted that not every board reaches this stage. Maturity is a relative matter and change sometimes locks a board into the permanent turmoil of adolescence or young adulthood. The Corporate Person may also regress to previous stages as board and executive leaders come and go. With changes in membership and leadership, mistakes may be repeated. Behaviors may have to be learned all over again, unless good habits and culture have become an established part of the corporate personality.

However, the Corporate Person at mature middle age knows who it is and what it is doing. Clarity of mission, vision, and values are hallmarks of its maturity. They allow it to deliberate and make decisions with vigor and confidence. The board and its executive leader each understand their roles. There is a high level of trust that enables planning to be done with strategic goals, and implementation steps to be identified in terms of human and financial resources, established time lines, and methods for monitoring and evaluating. Policy provides for strong delegation of authority to the executive leader who, in turn, is clearly accountable to the board.

The board's meetings are well-organized and agenda-driven, with adequate preparation and information shared in advance. There is a high degree of reliance on the executive leader, staff, consultants, and technical experts for reports and recommendations. The board makes efforts to stay abreast of a changing environment and because of its commitment, knowledge, and full participation, it is able to respond quickly to challenges, crises, and change.

Yet the mature Corporate Person, at middle age, may discover that its very strengths bring potential for difficulty and danger. Confident in the way it functions, the board may seek to exemplify the idealized Fortune 500 corporate bodies of the proprietary world, so that mission and values are sometimes overshadowed by the perceived need to grow, expand, and increase its bottom line.

As new ventures, collaborations, and partnerships begin, and as management proposes new programs and services, there may be a distancing of the board from the information it needs to carry out its governance responsibilities. Monitoring and evaluation of programs and executive leadership become more difficult, and board self-assessment may be postponed because of the press of board business. The executive leader may assume power simply by virtue of the need for expertise and technical knowledge, and the board—no matter how mature—cannot keep pace.

When new ventures begin to be overwhelming, the board may be confronted with the hard choices of merger and consolidation, testing the political and economic realities of whether or not "bigger is better." Indeed, the Corporate Person may vote to change its identity, in the hope of new life in a totally different shape, form, purpose, and reason for being. However, if it retains its identity, the Corporate Person will either maintain its maturity in governing at middle age, revert to an earlier life cycle stage, or it may retire.

The honorary elder stage exemplifies the latter, for here the board exists mainly for certain honorary, ceremonial, or figure-head purposes. The Corporate Person as an honorary elder enjoys the distinction and status of lending the prestige and soliciting the financial contributions of its members, while regularly rubber-stamping the recommendations of staff. The fiduciary trust obligations and ethical and legal responsibilities are still there, but rarely discussed. Somewhat corpulent and retiring, the Corporate Person-elder has distanced itself to the point of being a macromanager. It has no involvement in planning and little awareness of the turbulent environment around it, and it expends little energy and minimum effort. Board members, like doting grandparents, attend "when they can," giving nodding approval to a younger generation of executive leadership for whom they provide applause and affirmation.

Obviously at this geriatric stage, the Corporate Person-elder loves to be associated with great programs and strong leadership. It may be a fine spokesperson for the organization in the community ("Let me tell you about my grandchildren!"), and a strong advocate with funding sources. That's true as long as the organization is running smoothly.

The problem comes when there is crisis; when the honorary elder—having done no monitoring, evaluating, or self-assessment—is confronted with either real sickness within the corporate body or real threats from the outside. At that point, the Corporate Person becomes aware of its mortality and radical steps must be taken for it to survive and be revived. Its only hope is to regain a stage of maturity and competence that it has allowed itself to grow beyond.

Continued renewal

Understanding the life cycles of the Corporate Person gives an organization's board and executive leadership the ability to look at the current stage of its life and anticipate what may be the stages of its future.

An evolutionary pattern of growth means that life is always in process. The five stages described above are obviously caricatures of the Corporate Person. In real life, boards are continually exhibiting characteristics, tendencies, and behavior patterns that overlap from one stage to another. Nevertheless, the patterns are there.

For the board member readers of this book, reflection on the health of their Corporate Person may be useful in several ways:

- If there are tensions, communication breakdowns, or symptoms of stress from internal malaise or external threats, recognition of life cycles may help to explain why.
- Understanding stages of growth may help to identify adjustments and corrective action that is needed to move beyond a certain stage to more vigorous life.
- When the stress and pain of change, challenge, and crises appear, it's helpful to know that in the life cycles of the Corporate Person such symptoms are a normal and inevitable concomitant of growth, and not necessarily a sign of incompetence or pathology.

Even in what appear to be chaotic situations, there are "natural processes that support the quest for structure, process, renewal, and integrity."[12] That gives great hope to the members of the Corporate Person. It gives a reason throughout its life to strive for a healthy body for service, a healthy soul for vision, a healthy mind for intelligence, healthy behavior for integrity, and a strong, healthy voice to affirm its mission.

Questions for discussion
Chapter 7: Health

1. Health for the Corporate Person means expending effort to work for wholeness and build new vitality. (p. 65)

    A. As a Corporate Person, how does the board of which you are a member react to pain? Does your board resign itself to suffering without doing anything to correct the situation, or has your board experienced growth through pain?

2. The mature group is willing to examine itself. . . . The healthy group must assume responsibility for diagnosing its own problems and changing its procedures or processes. (p. 66)

    A. What is your board's process for self-assessment? When was the last time it was done?

    B. Who has the responsibility for managing the self-assessment process for your board?

3. If the Corporate Person is really healthy, what should the vital signs look like? (p. 70)

    A. What vital signs has your board found useful as criteria for measuring the health of your Corporate Person?

4. What brings stability and strength when the winds of change blow so hard that they threaten the life, health, and well-being of the Corporate Person? The operative answer is *organizational continuity*. (pp. 72–73)

    A. What is your board doing to foster and sustain relationships with your stakeholders and constituents?

    B. What is the ongoing planning process that gives your board continuity of policy and programs in the midst of a changing environment?

    C. How is quality assurance measured and monitored by your board?

    D. What is your board's role in the recruitment and nomination of new board members? What is your board doing to ensure the quality of future board leadership?

    E. What are the policies for executive succession in your organization?

5. For the Corporate Person, the change from one stage of life to another happens . . . (p. 75)

    A. Where in the Corporate Person's life cycle do you see your organization?

Notes

Chapter 1:

The Encyclopedia Americana International Edition, 1994 ed., s.v. "corporation."

1. "In 1245 the Roman Catholic Church, to articulate this concept, used the term 'corpus' from which has evolved the term 'incorporate' (to make into one body). The Church, itself a superb example of an undying owner of considerable temporal property, was always represented by some natural person." *Collier's Encyclopedia*, 1993 ed., s.v. "corporation."

2. "The corporation developed from the practical and intellectual difficulties of determining what was 'church land.' The English lawyers of the thirteenth century were not at all sure who owned church property. Under Roman law, church property was under a system whereby ownership was centralized, administered by the bishop. The village churches and the clergy received the benefits of ownership and use only as the bishop permitted. . . . In the thirteenth century, Pope Innocent IV permitted the development of the local church corporation as an artificial legal entity. On October 5, 1279, Edward I, king of England, approved the granting of charters ('articles of incorporation') to congregations of local parishes, giving governmental recognition to ecclesiastical corporations." Eugene Hackler, "The Ecclesiastical Corporation As A 'Legal Person,'" paper written for congregational councils of the Missouri-Kansas Synod of the Evangelical Lutheran Church in America, 3–4.

3. Roy J. Enquist, "A Paraclete In the Public Square: Toward A Theology of Advocacy," *Theology and Public Policy* 2, no. 2 (fall 1990): 23–24.

4. *Funk and Wagnalls Standard Reference Encyclopedia*, 1959 ed., s.v. "corporation."

5. William Barclay alludes to this idea, referring to the comments of Sir William Ramsey on that subject, in an essay on the word *ekklēsia* in *New Testament Words* (Philadelphia: The Westminster Press, 1974), 71.

6. *Westminster Dictionary of the Bible*, 1944 ed., s.v. "church."

7. Barclay, *New Testament Words*, 69.

8. *The Encyclopedia Americana International Edition*, 1994 ed., s.v. "corporation."

9. Ibid.

10. Eugene Hackler, "Understanding The Basic Legal Concepts" (October 11, 1984), 16–17.

11. In not-for-profit circles, the board historically has been referred to as *trustees* because board members were invested with a trust responsibility to act on behalf of all the people of the corpus/body. The title "board of directors" emerged with proprietary corporations where private funds were to be governed by decision making in the stockholders' interest. Today the terms are virtually used interchangeably in not-for-profit organizations.

12. " . . . no matter how important (corporate) members may be, they do not control the affairs of the association; this is solely the function of the board. . . . This issue was addressed in the . . . case of *Simoni v. Civil Service Employees Association* (N.Y.) in which the membership adopted several resolutions ordering the board to take certain actions. The board refused, and the court upheld their right to do so, saying that the nonprofit corporation statute places management authority solely in the hands of the board. This is true of statutes in all states. Typically, these statutes provide as follows: 'The affairs of the corporation shall be managed by a board.' . . . Of course, members can exercise control through any voting or removal powers they may have, but they cannot manage the organi-

zation or dictate management policy to the board." Hugh K. Webster, ed., "Members May Not Dictate Policy," *Membership Organizations Newsletter* 1, no. 1 (1989): 1.

CHAPTER 2:

1. Richard O. Scherch, "A Congregational Guide to Strategic Planning" (Sarasota, Fla.: Building Bridges, 1992), 2.

2. See chapter 3 for a further development of this theme.

3. John Carver, "A New Design for Governance" (workshop presented at the Triennial Conference of the Division for Social Ministry Organizations, Evangelical Lutheran Church in America; Chicago, Ill.; April 28, 1990.)

4. John Gardner, *On Leadership* (New York: Macmillan Inc., 1990), 95.

5. John Carver, *Non-profit and Governmental Boards: New Design for Leadership* vol. 2, segment 5 (Carmel, Ind.: Carver Governance Design Inc., 1994), videocassette.

6. For an excellent elaboration of the principles of board and staff interaction, see "Six cardinal rules to help boards solve top management problems" by V. Clayton Sherman, *Trustee Magazine* 36, no. 10 (October 1983): 40.

7. See chapter 5 for more on the behavior of the Corporate Person.

8. Webster, "Members May Not Dictate Policy," 1.

9. "Agency" refers to the idea that the board would act simply as an agent for the corporate members who insist on the right to retain control and final say over all board actions. If the corporate membership demands that kind of control, the risk of ascending liability to all of the corporate members is greatly increased.

10. From a speech by Monsignor Charles Fahey, director of the Third Age Center, Fordham University, N.Y., presented at the 1985 Conference of the American Association of Homes for the Aging, Los Angeles, Calif., 1985.

11. Ibid.

12. See chapter 3 for further discussion on this issue.

13. Andrew Swanson, *Board Sense*, no. F-33, (Rumford, R.I.: Community Services Consultants, 1988).

14. Dan Cain, of the Cain Consulting Group, has written in an unpublished article for the Division for Church in Society of the Evangelical Lutheran Church in America: "Recruiting is easier when there are fewer board members to recruit. The trend in board size is to smaller boards of five to nine members. Boards that have downsized to that level are finding not only easier recruiting, but more commitment from a smaller board as well. A five- to nine-member board is big enough to bring a variety of perspectives to board deliberations, but small enough to be manageable, less expensive to operate, and more involved. Smaller boards generally show more commitment to the job, attend meetings more faithfully, communicate better, and work better as a team. A large board loses the personal feelings of ownership and responsibility that each board member must have to get fully involved with the big job of governing." Cain, "Limit Terms of Board Members" (Hawarden, Iowa: Cain Consulting Group, P.O. Box 272, 1991), photocopy, 3.

CHAPTER 3

Alexis de Tocqueville, *Democracy in America*, vol. II (New York: Vintage Books, 1945), 9, as quoted by Os Guinness in *The American Hour: A Time of Reckoning and the Once and Future Role of Faith* (New York: The Free Press, 1993), 152.

1. Donald R. Johnston, "Creating Tomorrow's Vision Today," *Trustee* 47, no. 3 (March 1994): 24.

2. Max De Pree, *Leadership Is An Art* (New York: Doubleday, 1989), 78–79.

3. The list of value words commonly used in not-for-profit organizations is extensive. Some most commonly used are: accountability, advocacy, altruism, caring, citizenship, excellence, fairness, faith, fidelity, honesty, inclusiveness, integrity, loyalty, respect, spirituality, and stewardship.

4. Peter Drucker, *Managing the Nonprofit Organization* (New York: HarperCollins Publishers, 1990), 45.

5. Comments made by Winifred Hageman at the 1991 Peer-Mentor Gathering sponsored by the Board Development Services program of the Division for Social Ministry Organizations, Evangelical Lutheran Church in America.

6. Independent Sector, "Profiles of Excellence: Studies of the Effectiveness of Nonprofit Organizations" (Washington, D.C.: Independent Sector, October 1989).

7. Anne Wilson Schaef and Diane Fassel, *The Addictive Organization* (New York: Harper and Row, 1988), 123.

8. Robert Greenleaf, *Trustees As Servants* (Cambridge, Mass.: Center for Applied Studies, 1972), 10–11.

9. Peter D. Bell, *Fulfilling the Public Trust* (Washington, D.C.: National Center for Nonprofit Boards), as quoted in "Why Boards Sometimes Fail to Act Accountably," *Board Member* (November–December 1993): 3.

Chapter 4

Peter Drucker, "Establishing Leadership," *A Practical Guide to Mission Application: From Mission to Operational Effectiveness*, (St. Paul, Minn.: InterHealth organizations, January 1994).

1. Stephen Covey, *The Seven Habits of Highly Effective People* (New York: Simon & Schuster, 1989), 261ff.

2. John Carver, "When Owners are Customers: The Confusion of Dual Board Hats," *Nonprofit World* 10, no. 4 (July/August 1992): 14.

3. Ibid, 15.

4. De Pree, *Leadership Is An Art*, 51.

5. From a speech by Glenn Tecker presented at the October 1986 conference of the American Association of Homes for the Aging, New York, N.Y.

6. Antony Jay, "How To Run A Meeting," *Harvard Business Review*, no. 76240 (March–April 1976): 121–122.

7. "Appropriate communication" means discussion of issues and concerns for the sake of gathering and sharing information. It does not mean "decision-swaying rump sessions" among an inside group of board members, pressuring executive leaders, or attempting to micromanage administrative work.

8. Peter Drucker, *Post-Capitalist Society* (New York: HarperCollins Publishers, 1993), 193.

9. Tecker, 1986 conference of the American Association of Homes for the Aging.

10. Guinness, *The American Hour*, 148, 158–159.

11. Jay, "How to Run a Meeting," 122.

12. From a speech by Andrew Swanson presented at the at the April 1989 conference of the American Association of Homes for the Aging, Washington, D.C.

13. Stuart L. Entz, *Director Handbook* (Topeka, Kan.: Business Press Inc., 1982), 31.

14. Karl Mathiasen III, "No Board of Directors Is Like Any Other: Some Maxims About Boards," (Washington, D.C.: Management Assistance Group, 1982).

15. Peter Senge, *The Fifth Discipline: The art and practice of the learning organization* (New York: Doubleday/Currency, 1990), 237–238.

Chapter 5

De Pree, *Leadership Is An Art* , 78–79.

1. Under the 1996 Taxpayer Bill of Rights (with reference to IRS Code, Section 6672—Responsible Person Penalty), this legal liability has been relaxed to some extent. "Unless there is no other person liable for the penalty, the penalty for failure to collect or pay over tax does not apply to an unpaid, volunteer board member of a tax-exempt organization if . . . he or she is solely serving in an honorary capacity . . . does not participate in the day-to-day or financial operations of the organization . . . [and] does not have actual knowledge of the failure on which the penalty is imposed." Internal Revenue Service, *Highlights of 1996 Tax Changes* publication 553, cat. no. 15101G (Washington, D.C.: 1996), 24. It should be noted that this provision cannot operate so as to eliminate all responsible persons from liability.

2. Larry D. Lauer, "Using Your Organization's Culture to Build Productivity and Reputation," *Nonprofit World* 11, no. 6 (November/December 1993): 34–35.

3. Thomas P. Holland, Richard P. Chait, and Barbara E. Taylor, "Institutional Governance: Identifying and Measuring Board Competencies" (study conducted by the National Center for Post-secondary Governance and Finance, University of Maryland, 1988–1990), as quoted in Susan K. Houchin, "Two Perspectives on Power and Leadership: Boards and Power," *The Trustee Educator* 6, no. 2 (summer 1995): 5.

4. Gardner, *On Leadership*, 97–98.

5. Patricia Dutcher-Walls, "Political Correctness, the Reformed Tradition, and Pluralism," *Theological Education* XXIX, no. 2 (Spring 1992): 80.

6. De Pree, *Leadership Is An Art* , 77–78.

7. In common parlance today, the title is frequently interpreted as synonymous with "board of directors," although legally there are quite clear distinctions. The "board of directors" title is more commonly associated with proprietary or investor-owned corporations, and carries with it less stringent trust obligations. The classic legal case for not-for-profit boards was the so-called Sibley Hospital case (*Stern v. Lucy Webb Hayes National Training School for Deaconesses and Missionaries*), in which Judge Gesell evaluated board members' actions against the standards established for corporate directors rather than against legal standards for trustees—an important distinction, because the hospital board has called itself a "board of trustees."

8. The legal rule is: "A willful and continued failure of a director to attend meetings of the board is a violation of a director's fiduciary duty, as a failure to exercise the care and prudence of a director." Hugh K. Webster, ed., "Absent Directors," *Membership Organizations Newsletter* 1, no. 12 (Aug. 9, 1990): 1.

9. Greenleaf, *Trustees As Servants*, 23.

10. Richard P. Moses, "The Obligation of Trusteeship," *Trustee* 45, no. 5 (May 1992), 24.

11. For most not-for-profit organizations (some church-related organizations have contested the rule), this document containing certain information including executive compensation and other tax-related matters is to be available to the public during regular

business hours at the organization's main office and branch offices with three or more employees. According to the National Center for Nonprofit Boards, "If there is something in the 990 that you don't want made public, you have a much bigger problem."

12. Greenleaf, *Trustees as Servants*, 11–12.

13. Carver, *Non-profit and Governmental Boards*.

14. Sherman, "Six cardinal rules to help boards solve top management problems," 40.

15. Margaret J. Wheatley, *Leadership and the New Science: Learning about Organization from an Orderly Universe* (San Francisco: Berrett-Koehler Publishers Inc., 1992), 22–23.

16. Ibid., 133.

17. John Carver is the leading proponent of policy governance, as articulated in his book, *Boards That Make A Difference: A New Design in Nonprofit and Public Organizations* (San Francisco: Jossey-Bass, Inc., 1990).

18. Susan K. Houchin makes this important observation about individual board behavior: "An individual serving on a board of trustees who is accustomed to the responsibilities and powers of an authorized position may have a difficult time switching gears when he or she enters the board room. Used to giving direction and having others act promptly upon it, the trustee who comes from a position of power and authority in their work may not value or possess the kind of skills necessary in a consensus-building process. The slowness of consensus-building can be frustrating for such a person. They may not feel that their contribution to the board is needed or even wanted." Houchin, "Two Perspectives on Power and Leadership," 5.

Chapter 6

Carver, *Boards that Make a Difference*, 186.

1. "Sales Tax Oversight . . . Panel Wants Knowledgeable Member Out," *Tulsa World*, July 26, 1990.

2. It should be noted that the principle of the corporate voice applies particularly to private not-for-profit boards whose essential unity is built around commitment to a common mission and purpose, unlike public organizations where election of individual members by a certain group of constituents requires an obligation to speak only for and be accountable only to that group (such as city councils, school boards, or state legislatures). While there are not-for-profit volunteer boards still organized on an association model, with members representing only those who elect them, the need for effective governance has required a move toward the corporate model, as described in this book by the metaphor of the Corporate Person.

3. Peter Brinckerhoff, "How to Survive a Business Start-Up in an Era of Scrutiny," *Nonprofit World* 12, no. 5 (September/October 1994): 18.

4. Andrew Swanson, *Board Sense*, no. 11, (Rumford, R.I.: Community Services Consultants, 1990).

5. Char Mollison, "Improving Bad Attitudes on the Board," *Strategic Governance* 2, no. 2 (December 1996): 1–2. Mollison cites particular sounds of rude voices:
- making sarcastic remarks about the views expressed by other board members
- taking as a personal slight or refusing to accept decisions or actions that didn't go one's way
- gossiping bout, second-guessing, or in some other way maligning staff
- encouraging or creating factions on the board
- interrupting or jumping into the discussion so quickly and so often that quieter board members stay silent

- making insinuations that others can't be trusted or have personal motives for their actions or views

6. Carver, *Boards That Make A Difference*, 187.

7. John Carver, "The CEO and the Renegade Board Member," *Nonprofit World* 9, no. 6 (November/December 1991): 15.

8. Sherman, "Six cardinal rules to help boards solve top management problems," 40.

9. William R. Conrad Jr. and William E. Glenn, *The Effective Voluntary Board of Directors* (Athens, Ohio: Swallow Press, 1976), 106.

10. Adapted from G. Worth George, "Leadership Jazz: Selected Themes for Orchestrating Nonprofit Quality," *Nonprofit World* 11, no. 2 (March/April 1993): 31.

Chapter 7

Wheatley, *Leadership and the New Science*, 18.

1. Ibid.

2. According to group-dynamics scholar L. Bradford (*Making Meetings Work: A Guide for Leaders and Group Members*, [LaJolla, Calif.: University Associates, 1976]) there are a number of clues that characterize dysfunctional groups. These include conflict within the group, polarization, apathy, avoidance of the task, difficulty in reaching decisions, ideas being attacked before they are fully expressed, and the manner in which the group reacts to the loss of old members and the entrance of new ones.

3. Mark L. Clark. "The Board of Directors As A Small Dynamic Group: A Review" *Administration and Policy in Mental Health* 16, no. 2 (Winter 1988): 94

4. Ibid., 96.

5. A paraphrase of John Carver's, "If you haven't said how it ought to be, don't ask how it is," from the paper "Monitoring" (Carmel, Ind: Carver Governance Design, 1989), 3–4.

6. While the terms "evaluation" and "assessment" are used almost interchangeably, the following distinction may be helpful: *Evaluation* is defined as "to identify the value," which happens when criteria and standards are established. *Assessment* is defined as "to measure the value," referring to the activity of checking actual performance against standards and criteria for measurement.

7. For a discussion of board evaluation and assessment, together with sample forms for measurement, see James M. Hardy, *Developing Dynamic Boards* (Erwin, Tenn.: Essex Press, 1990). Another excellent source of information, formats, and resources for board self-assessment is the National Center for Nonprofit Boards, Suite 510, 2000 L Street NW, Washington, DC 20036-4907.

8. The policies noted are from *The Executive Search Process: A Handbook For Use With Lutheran Social Ministry Organizations*, published by the Division for Church in Society, Evangelical Lutheran Church in America, 1992. Examples of policy wording:

Board Action for Executive Succession
In the event of (*title of executive position*) vacancy through resignation, retirement, death, or termination, the board will provide for interim management and be responsible for employment of a new (*executive*).

The chair of the board will see that a Search Committee is authorized by the board and will initiate the activity of that committee which will report its recommendations to the board.

Interim Management
In the event of a vacancy in the (*title of executive position*), the (*title of designated*

temporary leader) will serve in that capacity until the board is able to secure interim management.

The board will provide interim management during the executive vacancy either by appointing a staff person, contracting with an outside management organization, or employing an individual who is not currently on the staff or board of (*name of organization*).

Interim management services will be compensated at a rate mutually agreed upon between the board and the interim manager.

Interim management should be provided by the board as quickly as possible when a vacancy occurs in executive leadership.

(*NOTE: The chair of the board has an important leadership role with the board during a vacancy. Therefore, it is not appropriate for the chair of the board to assume the duties of the executive.*)

Internal Staff Promotion to Executive Position

All selection procedures and criteria for filing an executive vacancy shall be non-discriminatory and based on established criteria and qualifications. Upward mobility and promotion within staff will be considered in the search for executive leadership. Staff members will be given equal opportunity with outside applicants to apply for the (*title of executive position*) at the time of a vacancy.

Executive Job Description

The job description for the (*executive title*) shall be developed by the board in consultation with the (*executive*), and reviewed annually as a part of the (*executive*)'s performance review. A review of the (*executive*)'s job description shall also be undertaken by the board at the time of a vacancy in the (*executive*).

Executive Performance Review

An annual performance review and evaluation of the (*executive title*), will be conducted by the (*committee or other authorized group of board members*) in the month of _____.

The performance review will be based on the (*executive*)'s job description, mutually agreed upon goals and objectives for the past year, and performance standards established by the board. The purpose for an annual performance review is to:

1. inform the (*executive*) of the board's perception of his/her work and whether that work is meeting board expectations;
2. help the (*executive*) grow professionally and personally;
3. assist (*name of organization*) in fulfilling its mission more effectively through executive leadership performance; and
4. discuss compensation for the coming year.

9. Ichak Adizes, "Organizational Passages," *Organizational Dynamics Journal* (summer 1979): 4.

10. Karl Mathiasen III has written descriptively about board life cycles for the Management Assistance Group, 1935 K Street NW, Washington, DC 20006. This quotation is from Rebecca Leet, ed., "Understanding the Life Cycle of A Board," *Strategic Governance* 1, no. 1 (June 1995): 1.

11. Mathiasen, "No Board of Directors Is Like Any Other," 7–8.

12. Wheatley, *Leadership and the New Science*, 18.